D1147626

THIS BOOK SHOULD BE RETURNED ON OR BEFORE THE LATEST
DATE SHOWN TO THE LIBRARY FROM WHICH IT WAS BORROWED

AUTHOR	**CLASS**
HOLDING, N.H.	G I

TITLE
More sources of World War I army ancestry

More Sources of World War I Army Ancestry

Third Edition

NORMAN HOLDING

Illustrations by
DANDI PALMER

Published by the Federation of Family History Societies (Publications) Ltd.,
2-4 Killer Street, Ramsbottom, Bury
Lancashire BL0 9BZ, England.

First edition 1986
Second edition 1991
Third edition 1998

ISBN 1 18006 083 8

07768751

Printed and bound by the Alden Group, Oxford

CONTENTS

ACKNOWLEDGEMENTS

A book of this nature is really a compilation of information provided by others. It is therefore to those who helped by sending me details of many types of records and sources that my thanks should be given. Some 350 replies were received from Military Museums, County Record Offices and from individual family historians. These replies form a separate book but much of the information given has been used in the writing of this volume. To all those who took the trouble to reply to my questionnaires may I give my thanks.

Several other names spring to mind for the help they gave: Roger Pritchard, Roy Batten, Terry Wise, Mike Chappell, Alistair Kennedy, Col. P.S. Newton, Major B. Mollo, J.M.A. Tamplin, Col. T.A. Cave, Peter T. Scott, Dr. Carruthers, the late Brigadier F.R.L. Goadby and M. Willis. Without their knowledge and skills this book would have been very thin indeed.

I would also like to acknowledge the help given by the staff of The Imperial War Museum, Luton Central Library, The Public Record Office, Kew, The National Army Museum, the Ministry of Defence, the Ministry of Health and Social Security.

My thanks are due to Col. Iain Swinnerton and Pauline Litton for their careful checking of the draft and their helpful corrections. I am also grateful to Dandi Palmer for her excellent illustrations.

Figures 1 and 7 are reproduced with kind permission of the Trustees of the Imperial War Museum.

INTRODUCTION

Since the writing of *World War I Army Ancestry,* I have continued my researches into the field, firstly to try and find a little more about my own father's activities and secondly to satisfy my own curiosity. This book continues the list of sources mentioned in the first and is intended to be a continuation of that book. If he has not read a copy I feel that I should warn the reader that he may find this volume a little puzzling. I have written a very short summary as Section 1 but in no way does it meet the needs of the reader who starts from scratch. This book concerns itself with the minor sources of information, which, although they are few and far between, can, if one is prepared to use them, give valuable clues. As with more orthodox family history, one must have some knowledge of the social history of the time in order to understand what documents exist and where to find them. Hence, the chapter on Army history.

My own researches have prompted me to ask many questions, some of which I feel I have been able to answer, at least to my satisfaction. Others remain only partly answered and I feel it is not my job to carry out detailed research into what is a branch of military history. However, I have reported what I have found, quoted my sources and hope that someone will feel inclined to complete the investigation.

Apart from a few minor corrections and additions, I have included a few hints on the use of the Medal Rolls now in the Public Record Offoce, Kew Ref. No. WO329/... The Service records of WWI Soldiers and Officers are now becoming available, although only about 30% of the total still survive. Some information on these records has been added.

Norman Holding
February 1998

1

THE FIRST STEPS

Anyone involved in researching the history of a family involved with the First World War is faced with a task that at first looks easy but, before much progress has been made, comes up against many problems; not the least being the fact that so many soldiers' records were destroyed in the Second World War.

Most families have a collection of photos and other souvenirs of recent ancestors who fought in the war but enquiry produces very little in hard facts. It is often assumed at first that the soldier fought in the front line as a member of an infantry regiment; however, probably less than 40% can claim that distinction. The rest were part of the vast army who supplied both food and ammunition, looked after the wounded, repaired the roads and performed the multitude of tasks needed to keep some 3,000,000 men in France.

The obvious first step would most likely be to trace the ancestor's records. It is here that the first signs of a difficult task begin to dawn on the researcher.

When a soldier left the Army, his records were kept by his old regiment or corps for a number of years and were then forwarded to a central archive for storage. It was here that nearly all the records of WWI soldiers were collected. This store in Anside Street, Southwark, London (it was previously known as Walworth) contained some 1,900 tons of documents housed on 15 miles of shelving. Besides the records of millions of soldiers, there were also 250,000 files and 5,000 boxes of War Diaries. In 1940, this store was bombed and some 6 million records of men who had been discharged before 1939 were damaged in the resulting fire. Less then 30% of the records survived although these alone still require 11,000 ft of shelving, and most of them are in a very bad state, being charred around the edges and the writing smudged by water. Among the other documents lost were duplicates of War Diaries but fortunately the originals of these were stored elsewhere, having been used to write the *Official History of the War.* These Diaries are now in the PRO, Kew (WO95/. . .). Some of the records lost were from before the Great War and hence those with ancestors who served in the Boer War also have difficulties. Most of the other pre-war records that survived are now in the PRO, Kew. An earlier fire had destroyed the records of Victorian soldiers who had died while serving. Thus the files of soldiers' documents (PRO Kew W097/. . .) include only those discharged with a pension and do not extend beyond 1913.

The surviving soldiers records − the 30% − are joined by a smaller batch which contains details of those men who were involved with a pension of some kind. These were apparently stored elsewhere and hence escaped damage. These men were discharged with injuries, or died during the period 1914—20. As many men are listed in both sets, and the batch of burnt documents covers a period from the turn of the century up to 1939 the chance finding any trace of a World War I soldier appears to be between 1 in 4 and 1 in 5.

Records of soldiers that have survived are now becoming available at the Public Record Office, Kew. The so-called 'unburnt documents' are in Class WO364/. . . These represent about 8% of the total number of soldiers and were obtained from the Pensions Office to replace the originals which were destroyed by fire in 1940. Film of the 'burnt docs' are in WO363/. . . and will not be completely released until filming is completed in about 2000. (By June 1998, names with initials Z, X, V, U, Q, O and N as well as E have been released. D, C, B and A will follow slowly but the rest will have to wait for further funds to be made available. In total there are 33,000 boxes of documents to be filmed.) These 'burnt docs' represent only 20% of the total, the remaining 70% having been lost for ever. Records of officers are now available in Class WO339/. . ., WO374/. . . and with indexes in WO338/. . . With officers' records, the original documents are available although about 10% have been lost and the rest have been weeded.

While filming continues, the Ministry of Defence is prepared to search the originals for a fee. It is no longer necessary to prove a relationship to the soldier.

The records are filed in a variety of ways; in order that the Ministry may locate a particular record it may be necessary to know the regiment, corps, regimental number, pension book number and, of course, the soldier's name. Thus if you want to request the Ministry of Defence to give you details of your ancestor's record of service, you must give **all the details about the soldier that you know** (but not photographs). You should write to

Ministry of Defence,
Army Search CS(RM)2,
Bourne Avenue,
Hayes,
Middlesex, UB3 1RF.

Enquiries can only be dealt with by letter — there is no public access to records under any circumstances and pressure of work may delay a reply. A charge of £20 (1998) will be made for all enquiries, which is non-returnable in the event of no record being found.

Even when you are lucky enough to get the ancestor's record, it often does not give enough detail to identify the precise unit. That is with which of a regiment's tens of battalions, with which of the Royal Artillery's hundreds of Brigades, with which of a corps thousands of companies the ancestor might have served. A soldier's file would normally contain many documents but as many have been destroyed, a complete set on any one man may not now exist, thus further restricting the information available. The main method to resolve this problem is to gather together from family sources as much information as possible in order to construct sets of data. Each set of data should contain a date element and a location element. The more precise the data, the better. The fact that the ancestor fought in a certain battle will give both elements. The fact that he was gassed will provide a number of possible sets, each one of which is quite precise (*see Section 10*). Letters are a great help but photographs less so, unless they are both dated and marked with a location.

The next step is to trace a unit out of the approximately 5,000 which meets both the family tradition — 'he drove lorries full of shells' — and matches two or three sets of data. To do this, one must first read the histories of the war and those of the appropriate corps and regiments so that you are well aware which units carried shells or matched whatever clues other associated family tradition provides. Then analyse the movements of all possible units to locate those that match the data sets you have collected, i.e. they are in the right place at the right time. This work will need a study of Becke's *Orders of Battle* (Bibl. Ref. 6), *Orders of Battle GHQ* (Bibl. Ref. 3) and, particularly in the case of the Artillery and the Corps an analysis of the movements of all possible units by means of the numerous printed books given in Bibl. Ref. 10.

The rest of this book will help analyse the various documents still extant in order to obtain the best sets of data from them. The following Table 1 gives a number of typical family clues that may be interpreted to provide a set of data, i.e. date element plus location element. In some cases the unit or a group of units may be identified directly.

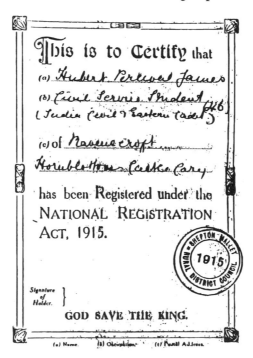

8

TABLE 1

Available Family Source	Method of Interpretation	Data Element that may be derived
Medals	Books	Rough Date
	London Gazette	Precise Date
		Major Unit
		Actual Unit
Documents		
Discharge Certificate	Army List	Actual Unit
Name of C.O.	Search of War Diaries	Actual Unit
Family Tradition		
Name of Battle	*Orders of Battle,* Becke	Rough Location
	(Bibl. refs.3 and 6, Sect. 1)	Possible Units
		Date
Name of Town	Official History	Rough Location
		Possible Units
Name of Country	Official History	Rough Location
(other than France)		Possible Units
Type of Job	Corps Histories	Type of unit
Regiment	Regimental History and	Possible Units
	E.A.James (Bibl. ref.1, Sect. 1)	
	Corps Histories	
Corps	Corps Histories	Many Possible Units
Wounded	Medical Records	Precise Unit
		Precise Date
Gassed	Medical Records	Possible Locations
		Possible Dates
Killed	*Soldiers Died in the Great*	Precise Date
	War, HMSO	Major Unit
Dates		Possible Locations
Deduced date for	Monthly Returns WO73	Possible Units
going overseas or at a	Weekly Returns WO114	Possible Dates
camp in UK		
At a place overseas	War Histories	Possible Units
	Orders of Battle	Possible Dates
	(Bibl. refs. 3 and 6, Sect. 1)	Possible Locations

Available Family Source	Method of Interpretation	Data Element that may be derived
Letters (continued)		
Dates		Dates
Cryptic Clues	Close examination of text of letter	Location
		Unit
		Date
Home Address	Electoral Roll Absentee Voters List	Precise Unit
Unit Address (on a letter to the soldier)		Precise Unit
Postmark	Postal History	Date
		Major Unit
		Location
Censor Stamp	Postal History	Precise Unit
Newspapers		
Local and National		Date
		Major Unit
Death	No interpretation required	Possible Date
		Major Unit
Leave		Possible Date
		Major Unit
Wounding		Possible Date
		Major Unit
Tribunal Report on Call Up		Date of Joining
Printed Books		
Village Record of Service		
Church Magazines		
War Memorials		Major or Actual Unit
Regimental Rolls		Date of Joining
School Rolls		also 'home town' or
Factory Rolls		other details such as
Town Rolls		school or place of work
Postcards *(see also Letters)*		
View of what?	Consult expert	Very rough Location
Name of Town		Rough Location
Name of Town cut out	Picture Postcard Books and Catalogues	Rough Location

Available Family Source	Method of Interpretation may be derived	Data Element that
Photographs of Soldier *(see also Letters)*		
Uniform	Books (Sect. 13) Rough Date	Possible Unit
Badges	Books (Sect. 13) Major Unit Rough Date	Possible Unit
Job (as seen in photo) General Books	Official Histories Possible Units (Types)	Rough Date
Where taken		Location
Background (of views)		Rough Location
Date		Date

Bibliography

General books on the British Army and its records which can be used to locate units.

(1) Garrison, Reserve and Veteran Battalions and Companies, by A.S. White, in *Society for Army Historical Research Journal,* Vol. 38, 1960.
(2) *British Regiments 1914–18,* by Brigadier E.A. James, Samson Books Ltd., 1982.
(3) *Orders of Battle GHQ,* PRO, Kew WO95/5400 et seq.
(4) The New Army Divisions, by Colonel T. Cave, in *Stand To,* No. 9, the Journal of the Western Front Association.
(5) The Territorial Infantry Division, by Colonel T. Cave, in *Stand To,* No. 8, the Journal of the Western Front Association.
(6) *Order o Battle of Divisions,* by Major A.F. Becke, HMSO, London, 1945. Parts 1, 2a, 2b, 3a, 3b and 4. Parts 1 and 2a reprinted by Sherwood Press, 1986/87. Parts 2b, 3a and 3b in one volume by Westlake Military Books, 1988/89.
(7) *Locations of British Cavalry, Infantry and M/C Gun Units 1914–24,* by R.T. Gould, circa 1978.
(8) Records of the Great War at the PRO, Parts 1 and 2, by P.T. Scott (Hon. Ed.), in *Stand To,* Nos. 6 and 7, the Journal of the Western Front Association.
(9) *The Location of British Army Records 1914–18,* by Norman Holding, Federation of Family History Societies, 3rd edn., 1991.
(10) *Lineage Book of the British Land Forces 1660–1978,* by J.B.M. Frederick, 2 volumes, Microform Academic Publishers.
(11) *Army Service Records of the First World War,* by Simon Fowler, William Spencer and Stuart Tamblin, 2nd edn., PRO Readers Guide No. 19, Public Record Office, Kew.

Periodicals

Many regiments published a journal which should always be sought out. *Stand To* is the Journal of the Western Front Association. Very good for contacting experts on a particular regiment or subject.

The Military Chest, bi-Monthly.
Military History and History Today.
Air Enthusiast, R.F.C.
The Army Quarterly and Defence Journal.
Cross and Cockade, Journal for the British Society of WWI Aero Historians.
Gallipolian, Gallipoli Association.
Boy David, Machine Gun Corps Association.
Guns, Weapons and Militaria.

2

THE BRITISH ARMY BEFORE AND AFTER 1914

In the early days of the British Army, the private soldier signed on for life and the regiments were numbered rather than named. They were originally formed by rich noblemen and landowners in the hope of favours from the king. Nicknames were given, such as the 'Green Howard's', which distinguished the Hon. Charles Howard's Regiment from George Howard's Regiment — one had Green uniform facings, the other Buff — hence the 'Buffs'.

The Army was organised around these regiments and there were few auxiliary services. These were in the hands of civilians or the Department of Ordnance.

In 1881 there was a re-organisation known as the Cardwell Reforms. The regiments not already having two battalions were grouped together in twos and given names which usually associated them with a county or other geographical area. The numbers were dropped, at least officially, and the new enlarged regiments were divided into two battalions each of around 1,000 men. As tradition dies hard in the Army, these battalions retained, at least as far as the men were concerned, the numbers given to their old pre-1881 regiments and more frequently its earlier name, particularly if this had some geographical or historical significance. A typical example was the 43rd Foot, known as the Monmouthshire Regiment and the 52nd Foot, known as the Buckinghamshire Light Infantry or, in colloquial parlance, the 'Ox and Bucks'. In this case the Monmouthshires died without a trace. A further example is given in the title of a book published in 1929:

> *With the 38th in France and Italy — being the record of the doings of the 1st Battation of the South Staffordshire Regiment, 26th Sept 1916—26th May 1918,* by Lieutenant-Colonel A.B. Beaumans.

Here the old number, 'The 38th', is still referred to even after the 1914—18 War.

A few regiments had four battalions, viz.

      Worcestershtre Regiment
      Middlesex Regiment
      Kings' Royal Rifle Corps
      Rifle Brigade

Some regiments existed as Territorial Force (TF) units only and hence did not follow the normal rules, e.g. The London Regiment, which was formed in 1908, had 26 battalions at the start of the war.

Although most regiments had County names, the association with the County was sometimes tenuous and it was not necessary for a battalion to be stationed in the

County, although its depot might be there. Besides men from the lower working classes of the mainland there was a high proportion of Irishmen in the ranks of most regiments. Up to the 1870s these recruits tended to be strong young country lads who looked for some escape from the low pay of the farm worker. By the turn of the century the poor country lads had moved to the town and henceforth fewer recruits came from the farm.

Militia

Besides the Regular Army there was also the Militia. This was the old 'Constitutional Force', a force of local men to serve at Home, its strength in 1898 being 93,600 men against its establishment of some 125,000. Each Militia Battalion was based on the Regimental Depot and had a full-time training and administrative staff of about 30 officers and NCOs from the Regular Army. Men signed on for six years and had to complete six weeks training during which they received a £1 or £1 10s bounty plus normal Army pay. Each year there was a further 28 days training also at full Army pay rates. There were also some Militia Artillery Brigades, a few Fortress Engineers, some Submarine Miners and the 600 strong Medical Staff Corps. A large proportion of the battalions were formed in Ireland and attached to Irish Regiments.

The long summer training periods were not suitable for factory workers and a high percentage of the recruits were farm labourers who joined to see if they liked army life before signing on for the Regulars. They would be very young; one third were under 18. At the other end of the scale, a few old soldiers joined. Very few completed the full six years' service so that after deducting the 30% who joined the Regulars and the 50% who deserted or were discharged, only some 20% were still there after six years. A few of these joined the Militia Reserve who received an extra £1 per year providing they agreed to serve overseas in an emergency. The Militia formed the 3rd Battalion of the regiment but they only really existed as a force at the Annual Camp.

Yeomanry

The Yeomanry was far smaller and could be considered as volunteer Cavalry. In 1899 it was only some 12,000 strong divided into 38 regiments. The permanent staff was limited to about 150 officers and NCOs in total, again from the Regular Army. The men had to provide their own horses and although they had an allowance of £2 per man paid to the regiment, this was insufficient to pay for uniform, band and horses even for the permanent staff. Thus the Yeoman had to be a rich man and the force was almost a Gentlemen's Club, a fact borne out by the uniforms which were most splendid, and in some cases the officers were elected. They had various duties which included local defence, the putting down of civil disorder and acting as escort to the Sovereign.

They trained by regular meetings or drills plus a yearly eight-day compulsory training camp.

Volunteers

The last and largest of the auxiliary forces was the Volunteer Force. This covered all types of units including Artillery and Engineers. Perhaps the most famous was the Honourable Artillery Company. The training consisted of weekly meetings on Saturday afternoons and evenings with only a poorly attended non-compulsory annual camp. This was only made mandatory after 1901 and then only for new recruits. The men were, for the most part, married men, small shopkeepers, skilled men and some professional men. Because of its middle class origins, the Volunteers were not well trusted by the Militia. They had, however, good relations with the landed gentry at the War Office.

These auxiliary forces were for Home Service only and were 'part-time'. That is, the men were able to continue with their normal civilian jobs, except during training periods. On the outbreak of war they became full-time and some volunteered for overseas duty. During the Boer War numbers of men from the Militia, the Yeomanry and the Volunteers served in Africa alongside the Regular Army although, with the exception of a few Yeomanry Regiments, most were used as reinforcements or combined with other volunteers into special units such as the Imperial Yeomanry.

The 1908 Reforms

After the Boer War, Haldane's Reforms of 1908 brought further changes. Since 1870 men had been able to enlist for 'short' periods of 12 years. The Infantry 'signed on' for seven years with the Colours and a further five years with the Reserve. The same applied to Cavalry of the Line. The other arms had various terms of service depending on the need for their services during peacetime.

	Colours	Reserve
Royal Horse and Royal Field Artillery	6	6
Household Cavalry	8	4
Foot Guards	3	9
Royal Engineers	6	6
Drivers, Royal Engineers (these would be horse drivers)	2	10
Army Service Corps	3	9
Drivers, Army Service Corps	2	10
Army Medical Corps	3	9

The Reservists had to attend 12 days or 20 drills annually and were paid a retainer of about six pence per day. The Regular Army of this time was organised into six Divisions of Infantry and one of Cavalry plus those units stationed abroad in India and in other remote parts of the Empire.

The Regular battalions of each regiment were now the 1st and 2nd Battalions The 3rd and sometimes the 4th were allocated to a new force to replace the Militia. This was the Special Reserve (3rd Battalion) and Extra Special Reserve (4th Battalion). Suitable recruits were able to enlist straight into the Army Reserve and after a short period of full-time training (about six months) they joined the Special Reserve and returned to their normal civilian jobs. Unlike the normal reservists they did not receive Reserve Pay but got an annual Bounty plus pay at Army rates during the 15 day annual training. The Special Reservists were based at the Regimental Depot and had their initial training there under their own officers but rarely met the Regular Army Reservists. On mobilisation those men from the Regular Reserve not required to bring the first two battalions up to a war footing would be included in the Special Reserve Battalion with the Special Reservists. It was intended that this battalion should provide a pool of trained men to reinforce the first two and its members had to agree to serve overseas on garrison duties during any war.

The old Militia was not disbanded but no new recruits were taken on and most of the force transferred to the Special Reserve. Within a few years the Militia had faded away. The initial turn of duty was six years but could be extended by four year increments up to the age of 40. The Special Reserve numbered about 70,000 men while, by 1913, the old Militia had dropped to some 700.

The same reforms brought an end to the Volunteers. In their place Haldane formed the Territorial Force (TF). In order to placate the old 'county' establishment, the TF was administered by County Associations who had to recruit and clothe the units under their care. For this they received a grant from the War Office dependent on the number of men. Training, however, was under the direct control of the Army. The Associations consisted of the Lords Lieutenant, members of the TF, local trade unionists, businessmen and politicians. These local contacts helped with the granting of leave for training. The men, who had to be between 17 and 35 years old, could enlist for four years. Pay was the same as the Regular Army while the TF was in camp. In addition, their CO could dispense a further one shilling per day and there was a boot allowance when in camp which was held each year and was in addition to the 40 drills for first year recruits and 10 per year for the others. Failure to attend camp brought a £5 fine.

The old Volunteers were thus left with no alternative but to join the TF and soon its numbers had grown to 276,000 men although by the start of the war this had fallen considerably. The TF was organised in the same manner as the Regular Army with the Force divided into 14 Infantry Divisions complete with Artillery, Medical Corps, Nursing Service, Engineers, etc. The old Yeomanry was transferred almost intact as the Cavalry arm of the TF. There were some complaints about the poorer pay compared with the past. The County Associations were also given control of the Yeomanry and as both arms of the TF were local in origin, their records often found their way into CROs. The names of the 1908–14 units are commemorated in present day Territorial units, but these latter have very few records referring to their predecessors.

In 1909, a number of other reserve forces came into being, a Territorial Reserve, a Technical Reserve and a Veteran Reserve which became the National Reserve. The first two did not amount to a great number of men but the National Reserve, which was made up of old retired soldiers, reached 190,000 officers and men by 1913 and 350,000 by 1914. Many of these joined the Regular Army or the TF at the outbreak of war but the older men formed the nucleus of the Royal Defence Force. The terms Militia and Volunteers tended to be used unofficially for the new Special Reserve and TF Battalions up to the start of the war.

This, then, was the state of the Army in August 1914 when the war started.

Regular Army 1st Battalion	1st Battalion of the Regiment
Regular Army 2nd Battalion*	2nd Battalion of the Regiment

These to be reinforced by soldiers of the Regular Reserve.

Special Reserve**	3rd Battalion of the Regiment
Extra Special Reserve**	4th Battalion of the Regiment
The Territorial Force	5th Battalion of the Regiment
The Yeomanry Regiments	
The Territorial Force Reserve	
National Reserve	
Cadet Force units — retained from the old Volunteer Force	
Officer Training Corps Units — mainly attached to Universities	

* A few regiments had four battalions of Regulars. Subsequent battalions were two higher.
** Some regiments only, in other cases the Battalion numbers of subsequent battalion were one lower.

The Changes of 1914—18

On the 4th August 1914, the outbreak of the war, the Regular Army at home numbered some 270,000 including 145,000 Reservists. A further 100,000 men were overseas in India and the Colonies. Within a few days 70,000 men of the Reserve were called to the Colours and an Army despatched to France. Kitchener had little faith in the TF which numbered some 300,000 men and was at least partly trained. On the 7th August, he called for a 'new army' of 100,000 to be followed within weeks by three more 'new armies'. A total of 500,000 volunteered for service by mid-September. A large number of the TF were sent overseas to replace the Regulars who had been recalled from the outposts of the Empire. The need for men in the corps was particularly urgent — the Army Service Corps (ASC) had only some 6,000 men when the war started — and any man who could drive a lorry or mend a horse harness found himself in France within days of signing on at the recruiting office, with or without rifle drill. In the early days of the war old soldiers were taken back up to an age of 55 years in some skilled trades.

Kitchener's call brought queues of young men to the recruiting offices. In many towns committees were formed who enrolled local men into what were known as 'Pals' Battalions. These men were fed, clothed and housed by the committees until they were all taken over by the War Office in January 1915 and, in addition to a number, their battalion titles included a name indicating the town of origin. Records of some of the Town Committees have reached CROs and some towns printed lists of men in book form.

The half million men were formed into 326 battalions, 250 being designated as 'Service' battalions in addition to being allocated a Battalion number which followed on in sequence after Territorial Battalion(s) The remainder became 'Reserve' Battalions.

During the remainder of the war the continuing stream of volunteers and later conscripts required the formation of many new battalions. These had a variety of titles and often had no connection with the 'parent' regiment other than its name. New recruits were posted to any regiment which was under strength at that instant of time and little or no regard was taken of the recruit's preference or his county of origin. Many of these new Reserve Battalions were used for training purposes only and when trained the men were transferred to one of the other battalions which were now overseas. In September 1917, some of the new battalions were grouped together to form a Training Reserve of some 112 battalions without any regimental designation whatsoever. These provided reserves when the normal Regimental Reserve Battalions were unable to meet the need for trained men.

In May 1917, the Training Reserve was reorganised into two groups designated Young Soldier Battalions (14) for 18 year-old recruits and Graduated Battalions (28) to which they were transferred after basic training. Then in October 1917 these two groups were re-allocated to regiments and given designations of 51st and 52nd for the Graduated and 53rd for the Young Soldier Battalions irrespective of the numbering system used in the regiment. The remainder of the Training Reserve provided six Recruit Reception Battalions and four Machine Gun Corps Training Companies. These last two groups were themselves disbanded in early 1918.

The TF was called to the colours at the outbreak of war and volunteered en masse for overseas services. Initially a large proportion was sent to India but a few units were sent to France — a list can be found m the PRO, Kew WO158/931 — others went to Egypt. Later on, many TF units served in France and in Gallipoli. The TF units connected with the Corps and the Royal Artillery maintained their identity throughout the war with the exception of those of the ASC which were absorbed into the main body of the ASC in January 1915.

Most 1st Line Territorial Battalions changed their numbers from 4th (or 5th) to 1/4th (or 1/5th) in the first days of the war and formed Reserve Battalions and later additional Reserve Battalions These were designated '2/' or '3/' in front of the normal battalion designation, i.e. 2/4th or 3/4th. In April 1916 the 3rd line Battalions were renamed as Reserve Battalions, e.g. (Reserve) Battalion TF and given their own battalion number. Numbers of men of the 2nd and 3rd Line Territorial Battalions who had not volunteered for overseas service or were of a low medical grade were formed into Provisional Battalions. This took place in June/July 1915 but they were later disbanded. In January 1917, the Provisional Battalions became numbered Home Service Territorial Battalions in Infantry Regiments.

Other battalions were formed in Infantry Regiments from dismounted Yeomanry Regiments. These battalions had the Yeomanry Regiment title incorporated into their own name (Bibl. ref.13).

The requirements of the army for groups of workers at home and abroad led to the raising of Labour, Transport Workers (for dockwork; Dec 1916 and Feb 1917) and Pioneer Battalions Garrison Battalions (older or low medical grade men for service in overseas garrisons; Dec 1915) were also formed. These had their own series of numbers within the regiment, i.e. 1st Garrison Battalion, 2nd Garrison Battalion, etc. The total number of battalions came to over 1760 and a short history of each one is given in *British Regiments 1914—18* by Brigadier E.A. James (Bibl. ref. 13). Details of movements and locations of home-based battalions can be found by careful analysis of *Commanders Home Forces 1916 and 1917, Officers in Command, Home Forces 1918, Officers in Command Forces in Greait Britain 1918 Distribution of Home Defence Troops and Reserve Units 1917 and 1918,* all published by GHQ (IWM) WO114/. . .; Weekly Returns of Regular and TF units in Great Britain (PRO, Kew); WO158/931 gives movements of TF units around Nov 1914 (PRO, Kew); *List of Land and Buildings in the Occupation of the War Department 1st June 1918* (NAM). Although some of these documents give numbers of men transferred on a certain date, no names are given. Thus it is impossible to trace a man as he moved from unit to unit during his training. By careful checking of postmarks, *Land in Occupation of the War Department,* and the other sources mentioned, it might be possible to guess at the man's movements but proof is impossible unless there is definite family information. The Electoral Roll of the Camp may give a man's name but not his unit. None of the few Nominal Rolls that survive deal with training battalions. TF Depots were given numbers and these numbers have been found on papers still in family hands. AC1 1496/July 1916 (PRO, WO293/5) identifies these numbers and gives a further clue to the ancestor's training camp.

There is yet another form of volunteer unit which sprang up in the wave of patriotism in August 1914. By November these were grouped together and given a grant as The Central Association of Volunteer Training Corps. A lovat green uniform was specified (see photo in Bibl. refs. 6 and 19). A red band was worn with the letters 'GR'. This was dropped in December 1916 together with the green uniform which was replaced with the serge uniform presumably in khaki colour. Administration passed to the County TF Association and from July 1918 the Volunteers became the Volunteer Battalion of the local regiment. Volunteers also had Field Ambulance and Motor Transport units. Records are often found in CROs and notices of parades with names of men appear in local newspapers.

The Royal Defence Corps was used to guard important points in the UK and consisted of older men, often of lower medical grade. During 1917, it took over a number of Home Service Garrison Battalions from the regiments but was originally formed from Supernumerary TF Companies in March 1916. It came under the London TF Association which was responsible for the corps for the whole country.

Bibliography

Pre-1914

(1) *For Queen and Country,* by Bryon Farewell, Allen Lane. A Social History of the Victorian and Edwardian Soldier. Hardly reached the period of WWI.

(2) *The Development of the British Army 1899—1914,* by J.K. Dunlop. The standard book on the subject(NAM).

(3) *The Saturday Night Soldiers,* by A.V. Sellwood, White Lion Publishers, London. The story oú the Territorial Force and the Yeomanry.

(4) *The Mons Star,* by David Ascoli, Harrap, London. Gives a brief outline of the Army just prior to 1914.

(5) *The British Army of 1914,* by Major R. Money Barnes, Seeley Service Co., London.

(6) *Hertfordshire Soldiers,* by J.D. Sainsbury, Hertfordshire Local History Council, 1969. Gives a history of the various arms of the force as applied to Hertfordshire.

(7) *The ABC of the Army,* by Captain J. Atkinson, Gale and Polden, London, 1914. A slim volume probably produced for recruiting in the pre-war years. Many precise facts about pay and terms of service (NAM).

(8) *His Majesty's Territorial Army,* by Walter Richards, Virtue and Co., 4 vols., 1910–11. A descriptive account of the Yeomanry, Artillery, Engineers and Infantry, etc.

(9) *An Annotated Bibliography of the British Army 1660—1914,* by A.P.C. Bruce, Garland Publishing Inc., 1975.

(10) The 'local' newspaper usually carried details of TF training meetings, camps, etc. Weekly orders were published therein and gave names of men.

Post-1914

(11) *Kitchener's Army and the Territorial Forces,* by Edgar Wallace, published by George Newnes Ltd., no date but about 1915. Many pictures, early recruiting and training.

(12) The New Army Battalions 1914—18, by Brigadier E.A. James, in *The Bulletin,* Vol. 22, p. 105, The Military Historical Society. Details of the forming of the Service Battalion(s).

(13) *British Regiments 1914—18,* by Brigadier E.A. James, Samson Books, 1978. A brief history of each Battalion, including Infantry, Cavalry and Territorial Force.

(14) *Locations of British Cavalry, Infantry and Machine Gun Units 1914—24,* by Robert W.Gould. A brief history of each Battalion as in ref. 13. Somewhat shorter but including Machine Gun Corps units.

(15) *The War in the Trenches,* by Alan Lloyd, Hart-Davies MacGibbon, 1976. The opening chapters give the background to early recruiting.

(16) *Hertfordshire's Soldiers,* by J.D. Sainsbury, Echo Press Ltd., 1969. Although this deals with the Hertfordshire Regiment (and its connection with the

Bedfordshire Regiment), it gives much detail on the various types of wartime battalion, including various auxiliary units.

(17) List of Territorial Force units arriving in France 1914—15. *The Journal of the Orders and Medals Research Society,* 1972, p.72.

(18) *The Fighting Territorials,* by P. Hurd, London Country Life, 2 vols., 1915—16.

(19) *The National Guard in the Great War 1914—18,* by A.E. Manning Foster, Cope and Fenwick, 1920, 304pp.

(20) *Extracts from about 200 Army Council Instructions dealing with the Volunteer Force 1916—19.* Clothes, badges, ages of men, young boys as buglers 14—17, etc. PRO, Kew, WO161/109.

(21) *The Voluntary Recruiting Movement in Britain 1914—16,* by J.M. Osborne, Garlar Publication, 1984(?).

(22) *The Defenders, a History of the British Volunteer,* by Geoffrey Cousins, Frederick Muller, 1968.

(23) *The Territorial Force 1914,* by Ray Westlake, 1988.

(24) *Kitchener's Army. The raising of the New Armics 1914—16,* by Peter Simkin, Manchester University Press, 1990.

3

REGIMENTAL NUMBERS

The ancestor's regimental number is one of the pieces of information that is usually available to the researcher. It was used on almost every item of paper dealing with the soldier and is also engraved on the rim of his medals.

When dealing with large numbers of people, common surnames occur frequently — often with the same Christian names, hence an additional means of identification was valuable. However, although the initial numbering system used by the Army in 1914 was adequate for a peacetime army, it could not cope with the vast increase of numbers brought about by the war. With care it might be thought possible to use the ancestor's number to deduce other details of his Army service, such as his approximate date of joining his regiment, but a careful study of the numbering system used by his own corps or regiment is essential if one is not to be completely misled. The following will act as a guide on which to base further research, but it appears to be a much neglected subject and the researcher will be very much involved in breaking new ground.

At the start of the war, each battalion had its own series of numbers which had started at No. 1 and went up to several thousand. The date of the issue of No, 1 varied with the regiment from 1829 up to the start of the war. Thus a regiment with two battalions would have two sets of numbers and a single number could identify two different men each of a different battalion. This led to the practice of putting the battalion number in front of the number, viz. 2-1234. (From May 1915 ACI 144/1915, this became one of the approved methods.) Each time a man changed battalions, a common practice, he could be given a new number, but this was stopped in May 1915. From then on soldiers retained their number when changing battalions within the same regiment as is shown by men serving in, say, the 4th Battalionn still having 3/... numbers. Other regiments used one series of numbers for all the battalions from the beginning or at least one series for the Regular Battalions. The Special Battalions and the TF Battalion(s) would also have had their own sequence. There is also evidence to show that some regiments allowed unallocated numbers (i.e. where the man had been transferred, been discharged or killed) to be given to new recruits. In addition, various Base camps in France and other overseas areas were allocated blocks of numbers from the regiments and corps so that men transferred to a fresh regiment whilst overseas could be given a new number straightaway. These blocks of numbers were supposed to be from a block of 5,000 above the normal range used by the unit at home. However, there were many misunderstandings and the rule was changed and any agreed block could then be used.

These variations made any deductions derived from the possible date of issue of the number completely worthless. The Corps, i.e. Royal Engineers (RE), etc. were each allocated a batch of six-fiqure numbers which could be issued throughout their corps and in January 1917 this series was extended by an added batch of six figures for each corps for TF units. A few months later, a similar system was introduced by the regiments but again only used for their TF men. The ASC had one series at least from December 1914 and in January 1915 all men of TF ASC units were given Regular Corps numbers.

This change was an improvement, but transfers between regiments or corps still meant a change of number and as six fiqures only allowed for 1 million men out of a maximum strength of two to three million, there were still duplications. It was not until 1921–2, after the war, when a new eight digit series was introduced, that this duplication was eliminated and that revision held until the start of the 1939–45 war.

There is no standard book dealing with this subject so the researcher must solve his own problems. The complexity of the system causes much misunderstanding and few records exist today to help in providing the answers. The bibliography gives several references to articles, mainly by medal collecting enthusiasts, which attempt to explain the situation but usually the most detailed articles apply to one regiment only (Bibl. ref.3). The Army Council Instructions — W0293/1 to 10 PRO, Kew — give the basic rules, but the indexing system used makes a reliable search of the many thousands of instructions very time consuming.

The various lists of men can be used by the researcher to estimate the date of joining the Army. By looking at the actual Registers of the Medal Rolls for a regiment in W0329/. . . PRO, Kew, one can see a nearly complete sequence of regimental numbers; only those who did not serve overseas are omitted. These Rolls do not, as a rule, give the date of joining but the notes in the last column often give an indication of that date: 'Transferred from Sussex Yeomanry 2/4/17' or similar remarks indicate when that number was first issued. Also those who died are frequently mentioned, with a date. That number must have been issued before the date of death. By looking at several pages it is possible to estimate the date at which batches of numbers were issued. As a further and more accurate check, a batch of about 50 or 100 names taken from above and below the ancestor's number can be cross referenced with the 14 volumes of *The National Roll of Honour* (Bibl. ref. 6) which can be found in the Libraries of the Imperial War Museum or the Society of Genealogists. *The National Roll of Honour* gives the date of enlistment and hence can be used to estimate when the ancestor enlisted even if he is not mentioned. As only a few men are included, a large number must be checked to find a match. One should always bear in mind that the number given in the Medal Roll may not be that given upon enlistment.

If the ancestor's unit was involved in heavy fighting, a large number of its members could have received the Silver Badge when they were discharged wounded. The Rolls of those receiving this badge are also recorded in the registers in W0329/. .

and, unlike other available records, these do give the date of enlistment. Hence, using the techniques outlined in the previous paragraph, they also can be used to estimate the date of joining.

To sum up, regimental numbers can only be of use if you are prepared to do a lot of research. Exceptions to this rule are:

RGA numbers over 300,000
RHA and RFA numbers over 600,000
RAMC numbers over 300,000
Yeomanry numbers over 30,000
RE numbers over 400,000
ASC numbers over about 5,000.

In these cases, more information can be gained from the sources listed on the next few pages. These sources name the units allocated batches of numbers.

Regular Army — pre-1914

King's Regulations of 1912, paragraph 1899, stated that each soldier was to be given a number. The range of numbers for each corps, regiment, etc. is stated. In November 1914 this was amended by Army Order 453/1914. This increased the maximum number that could be used by each unit. This maximum was far higher than the number of men expected to serve in the unit and hence this information is of very little use to the family historian.

Service Battalions

The introduction of a large number of men into the newly formed 'Kitchener' or, more accurately, 'Service' Battalions usually meant that the range of numbers used for the Regular Battalion was extended in the same sequence so that the new volunteers soon received numbers in the tens of thousands. This number usually stayed with the man when he changed battalions, but not when he changed regiments. To contradict this system, it is known that some regiments, for example the West Yorkshire Regiment, had a separate series for each battalion plus the battalion number as a prefix, e.g. 7-1352 was the 1352nd recruit to the 7th Battalion (Bibl. ref. 3e). From May 1915, all regiments had to use this latter system if they did not use one series for the whole regiment. TF Battalions had their own series.

Yeomanry Regiments

Each Yeoman Regiment had its own series of numbers, usually in the hundreds. On 1st April 1917, all Yeomanry were renumbered into one long sequence; thus all Yeomanry men had a different number no matter to which Yeomanry Regiment they belonged. This series began at 30,000. Many Yeomanry Regiments were later officially transferred to Infantry Regiments where they fought as infantry. These men lost their Yeomanry '30,000' series numbers and received '200,000 series TF numbers instead, but whereas the former series gave a unique number to each man, the latter was unique only within the regiment.

Yeomanry Lancers from 30,000 to 60,000
Yeomanry Dragoons from 70,000 to 180,000
Yeomanry Hussars from 200,000 to 335,000

ACI 381 3rd March 1917 Appendix 65, lists the batches allocated to all the Yeomanry Regiments and thus provides positive identification.

The Territorial Force

The Territorial Force, which was founded in 1908, had its own numbering system, again based on the battalion or the regiment, which means that a man in the Territorial Battalion (usually 4th or 5th) could have an identical number to a man in the Regular (1st or 2nd) Battalion. On 1st March 1917 (ACI 2414 Dec 1916), a new series of numbers was issued to men of the TF, now fully absorbed into the regiments. These started at 200,000 and were issued in batches of 40,000 to the Territorial Battalions of each regiment as follows: The 1st TF Battalion (usually the 1/4th or 1/5th Battalion of the Regiment) 200,001 to 239,999. The 2nd and 3rd line Battalions (i.e. 2/4th and 3/4th) would use the same sequence following on from the 1st line Battalion. The subsequent battalions, i.e. (1/5th, 2/5th and 3/5th) and any further battalions would be issued with numbers in the succeeding 40,000 batches, i.e.

240,000 – 279,999   1/5th, 2/5th, 3/5th
280,000 – 319,999   11th Battalion (TF) etc.

There appears to be some deviation from this rule.

(a) Men who were posted to a TF Battalion after receiving a number in the regiment's normal series while at a receiving or training depot did not always get a new '200,000' series number.

(b) In some regiments at, least, the later TF Battalions did not receive the full 40 000 batch of numbers. (The Highland Light Infantry issued the 7th, 8th and 9th Battalions with batches of 25,000 only – Bibl. ref.3k).

(c) Some men received the new numbers after they had been killed or, to be more accurate, the records that now survive show a 200,000 number for men who died before March 1917 (i.e. before the issue of the new numbers!).

A complete list of the batches of numbers allocated to TF infantry units is given in ACI 2414 Dec 1916 and in the appendix to that instruction.

ASC Numbers

At the outbreak of war, the Army Service Corps was very small and relied on Reservists to bring its numbers up to a war footing. This was still far too small for the requirements of the rapidly expanding Army so large numbers of men were encouraged to join the ASC by offering very high rates of pay. This caused much discontent among the old 'Regulars' of the ASC who, although paid more than the infantry, still received only a fraction of the rates of the new 'war period' recruits.

Pre-war Clerk	1s 4d per day (7p)
New recruit T/4 Clerk	4s 0d per day (20p)
Some highly skilled trades	6s 0d per day (30p) or more, e.g.
Fitters, Electricians	up to 7s 6d per day (37p)

Later on in the war, new recruits were restricted to about 2s 4d per day but the lucky few on 6s 0d and 7s 6d did not take a cut. The numbering system used in the ASC appears to have been a straightforward sequence which started before January 1915 at which date all men in TF ASC units were given numbers in that series which went up to over 400,000 by the end of the war. The series started at 1, the low numbers below 100,000 frequently being preceded by a nought. The date of the start is uncertain, but at the beginning of the war the ASC numbered less than 7,000 men of all ranks. By May 1915 they had reached 130,000.

The ASC is noted for its complicated system of letter prefixes to the number. These indicate the trade of the man. The ASC was split into four branches:

Remount	the department which procured and issued horses for the Army
Supply	dealt with all supplies
Transport	provided all the Army's transport requirements except those catered for by:
Mechanical Transport	the motorised branch of the Transport section.

These four branches had the prefixes R, S, T, or M. The addition of a second letter usually an 'S' denoted a man with special skills as opposed to a simple 'pair of hands'. For example

TS   Drivers (of a horse-drawn wagon)
      Saddlers
      Wheelers
      Farriers
      Shoeing Smith

The old pre-war Special Reserve had additional prefixes. These men were numbered in a pre-war sequence which ran from 1 upwards for each group, viz. TS and R, A, CHT, MS and SS. Due to the small size, the numbers would have been in the hundreds rather than thousands. When the new series started at the end of 1914, a new set of prefixes was introduced for new men but the old hands kept their old prefixes, although they may have been given new numbers. The new series was allocated to the four branches in batches of a few hundred up to a few thousand.

The first 300,000 numbers are shown in batches in Table 2. Table 3 gives a list of the ASC prefixes as taken from ASC documents.

The Royal Horse Artillery and Royal Field Artillery

The RHA and RFA used one combined series of numbers from 1 to 600,000 for Regular Soldiers and 600,001 onwards for TF Soldiers from 1st January 1917. ACI 2198/Nov 1916 (the Appendices) lists the batches allocated in individual TF units. A similar system was used for the Royal Garrison Artillery but in this case the change-over point was 300,000.

The Royal Flying Corps

Men enlisting before August 1914 had numbers below 1400.

The Royal Engineers

The RE used 1 to 400,000 for Regular and 400,001 onwards for TF units (AC12243/Dec 1916) from January 1917. Its Appendix lists TF units and batch numbers.

The Royal Army Medical Corps

The RAMC used 1 to 300,000 for Regulars and 300,001 onwards for TF units (ACI 380/March 1917) from 1st April 1917. Its Appendix lists TF units and batch numbers. See also ACI 470/1917.

Transfers

ACI 1245/1917 and the Appendix sets out the changes of Regimental Number when men were transferred.

The Machine Gun Corps

Formed 14th October 1915 with about 3,000 - 4,000 men. By 26th April 1916 the Regimental Numbers had reached 32,750 and increased at a rate of about 100 per day until September when the rate of increase became spasmodic (say 180,000 in September 1917).

General

Finally, remember that the number which is known to the researcher is often the one recorded in an official document and is not the one used by the soldier, at least not at the time that the document was published. There is plenty of evidence to show that *Soldiers Died in the Great War* gives numbers that were not issued to the soldier before he died and other cases where a medal refers to a number held by the man several years before he received the medal. In some cases it is possible to give an explanation for these discrepancies, but unless the researcher is fully aware of them, errors in deduction can be made.

Those awarded the 1914 Star or the 1914/15 Star would find it engraved with the regimental numbers that they held when they landed in France and thus qualified for the Medal. When, at the end of the war, they were presented with their British War and Victory Medals, these too would have the same number, even if they had changed it several times in the meantime. One qualified for the latter two by being in France and hence the number in use on the day of landing could be used, but this was not always the case (Bibl. ref 3e). Similarly, the term 'Lance Corporal' appears on some medals and not others. There is no need to speculate why the ancestor lost his stripe, it just depended on the subtle difference between a 'rank' and an 'appointment'. Lance Corporal was an appointment and as such was not always shown on documents and medals.

Post-1920 numbers

In 1920 a new system of numbering was introduced, when Regimental Numbers were replaced by Army Numbers. From that date a soldier was allocated a number depending upon the regiment or corps into which he enlisted. That number remained with him throughout his military career, no matter how many times he was transferred between regiments or even discharged and re-enlisted. This system continued up to the 1939—45 war. The new numbers were allocated to regiments in batches in a somewhat unusual order. The first batch went to the Royal Army Service Corps, ahead of the Life Guards and Royal Artillery. Whilst serving in the RASC a letter prefix (T, S, M or R) was added to the man's number.

A complete list can be found in Army Orders 338, 520 and 521 of 1920. A copy can be seen in PRO, Kew, W0123/62.

1–294000	Royal Army Service Corps
294,001–309,000	Life Guards and Royal Horse Guards
309,001–721,000	Cavalry
721001–1,842,000	Royal Artillery
1,842,001–2,604,000	Royal Engineers and Royal Signals
2,604,001–2,744,000	Foot Guards
2,744,001–3,377,000	Scots Regiments
3,377,001–6,972,000	English and Welch Regiments
6,972,001–7,245,000	Irish Regiments
7,245,001–8,109,000	All other corps. Womens' Services not included.

TABLE 2

Army Service Corps Regimental numbers
New Armies, Horse Transport (H.T.), Supply, Remount and Mechanical Transport (M.T.)

T	or	S/1	to	5400	H.T. or S.
		MI/5401	to	09400	M.T.
T	or	S2/09401	to	018400	H.T. or S.
		M2/018401	to	022400	M.T.
T	or	S3/022401	to	031400	H.T. or S.
		M2/031401	to	035400	M.T.
T	or	S4/035401	to	045500	H.T. or S.
		M2/045501	to	055500	M.T.
T, S	or	R4/055501	to	073000	H.T., S. or R.
		M2/07300	to	075000	M.T.
		DM2/075001	to	076000	M.T.
		M2/076001	to	083000	M.T.
T, S	or	R4/083001	to	096500	H.T., S. or R.
		DM2/096501	to	097500	M.T.
		M2/097501	to	106500	M.T.
T, S	or	R4/106501	to	112000	H.T., S. or R.
		DM2/112001	to	113000	M.T.
		M2/113001	to	122000	M.T.
T, S	or	R4/122001	to	129500	H.T., S. or R.
		DM2/129501	to	130500	M.T.
		M2/130501	to	134600	M.T.
		DM2/134601	to	135600	M.T.
		M2/135601	to	137600	M.T.
		DM2/137601	to	138600	M.T.
		M2/138601	to	139500	M.T.
T, S	or	R4/139501	to	144470	H.T., S. or R.
		RX4/144471	to	144560	R.
T, S	or	RX4/144561	to	146000	H.T., S. or R.
		RX4/146001	to	146100	R.
T, S	or	RX4/146101	to	147100	H.T., S. or R.
		M2/147101	to	151100	M.T.
		DM2/151101	to	151650	M.T.
		M2/151651	to	157100	M.T.
T, S	or	RX4/157101	to	158100	H.T., S. or R.
		RX4/158101	to	158300	R.

Table 2 *(continued)*

T, S	or	RX4/158301	to	162110	H.T., S. or R.
		DM2/162111	to	163200	M.T.
		DM2/163201	to	164220	M.T.
		M2/164221	to	164300	M.T.
		DM2/164301	to	166300	M.T.
		M2/166301	to	168300	M.T.
		DM2/168301	to	172110	M.T.
T, S	or	RX4/172111	to	174500	H.T., S. or R.
		M2/174501	to	176600	M.T.
		M2/176601	to	178600	M.T.
		DM2/178601	to	180600	M.T.
		M2/180601	to	182600	M.T.
		M2/182601	to	184500	M.T.
T, S	or	RX4/184501	to	187000	H.T., S. or R.
		M2/187001	to	189000	M.T.
		DM2/189001	to	191000	M.T.
		M2/191001	to	197000	M.T.
T, S	or	RX4/197001	to	200000	H.T., S. or R.
		M2/200001	to	206410	M.T.
		DM2/206411	to	210000	M.T.
T, S, R	or	RX4/210001	to	221000	H.T., S. or R.
		DM2/221001	to	221610	M.T,
		M2/2211611	to	223710	M.T.
		DM2/223711	to	225810	M.T.
		M2/225811	to	230010	M.T.
		DM2/230011	to	232110	M.T.
T, S, R	or	RX4/232111	to	264000	H.T., S. or R.
		M2/264001	to	266100	M.T.
		DM2/266101	to	266200	M.T.
		M2/266201	to	270300	M.T.
		M/270301	to	274500	M.T.
T, S, R	or	RX/274501	to	279000	H.T., S. or R.
		M/279001	to	299500	M.T.

By the end of the war, numbers up to 400,000 were being issued. The allocation of these is not known.

TABLE 3

ASC prefixes

TS	Old Army Transport Specials (own series of numbers before 1915) Divers Saddlers Wheelers Farriers Shoeing Smiths
R(?)/	Old Army — Remounts used TS/... sequence(?) Foreman Roughriders Nagsmen Strappers
A/	Old Army Special Reserve (own series of numbers before 1915) Drivers
CHT/	Old Army Special Reserve (own series of numbers before 1915) Roadmaster Foremen Wagoners
CMT/	Old Army Mechanical Transport (own series of numbers before 1915)
MS/	Old Army Mechanical Specials (own series of numbers before 1915) Workshop Foremen Electricians Drivers Fitters and Turners Blacksmiths Wheelers
SS/	Old Army Supply Specials (own series of numbers before 1915) Bakers Butchers Clerks
T(?)/ Transferred to T4/	Old Army Labourers used SS/... sequence(?) Foremen Gangers Privates

Table 3 *(continued)*

M/	Old Army (Mechanical Transport?)

T/1	
T/2	New Army Horse Transport
T/3	
T/4	

T/1SR	New Army(?) Special Reserve Horse Transport
T/2SR	

S/1	
S/2	New Army Supply
S/3	
S/4	

S/1SR	New Army (?) Special Reserve Supply
S/2SR	

R/4	New Army Remount
	Roughrider
	Groom
	Strapper
T/4	New Army Transport
	Cooks
	Batmen

M/1	New Army Mechanical Transport
M/2*	Electricians
	Fitters M/2 could be used as drivers

M1/1SR	New Army Mechanical Transport
M/2SR	Electricians
	Fitters (? Special Reserve)

M/1SR	New Army Mechanical Transport
M/2SR	Electricians
	Fitters (? Special Reserve)

DM/2*	Motor Driver Mechanical Transport Special 'Duration of War' enlistment for Motor Vehicle drivers

R x 4	New Army?

Unknown

NAC	?
RTS	Shoeing Smith
CAT	Driver

Table 3 *(continued)*

Although a new series of numbers was started about January 1915 and all 'old army' men appear to have been given new numbers, they retained their old prefixes except some T/ labourers who were given a T/4 prefix.

*Research on ASC men in Motor Ambulance Convoys leads one to think that many M2/... men were used to drive ambulances, as the number of M2's in the unit was far higher than the 12 fitters on the Establishment. Later, DM/2 were used.

Bibliography

(1) MH106/2386 *Archives chapters* and MH106/2389 *Location of Medical units, ASC Nos.*, PRO, Kew. Two sets of documents which give a brief explanation of the issuing of regimental numbers. These include a set of instructions to clerks searching medical records.
(2) IWM. *Paper on 1914 Medical Records,* by W.T. Thomason (316.22 80827). Explains the problems but not the systems, also PRO MH106/2387.
(3) *Journals of the Order and Medals Research Society.* Many references viz.
    a. 1972, March, p. 20. The Official Numbering System of the Royal Navy, by N.G. Gooding. Appears to be a very complete explanation.
    b. 1974, Winter, p. 194, by Major J.G.C. Macherson.
    c. 1975, Summer, p. 101, by R.L. Geach.
    d. 1975, Autumn, p.155, by I. Stedman. The Queen's Regiment, 1914–20. The result of seven years analysis of that Regiment's numbers.
    e. 1976, Summer, p. 82, by J.E.G. Hodgson. A good explanation.
    f. 1976, Autumn, p. 159, by B. Scott. The numbers of the Artists Rifles. This was almost entirely an Officers Training Unit and most members would be officers at a later stage of the war. A complete breakdown of the number system with dates of issue.
    g. 1976, Winter, p. 211. ASC prefixes.
    h. 1977, Spring, p. 37. A list of Army Council Instruction Numbers which apply to TF Numbers. ACI's are in the PRO, Kew under W0293/1 to ...
    i. 1978, Autumn, p. 143, by B.P. Connor. New Zealand Numbers, a complete breakdown.
    j. 1978, Spring, p. 41; 1979, Winter, p. 275, by Clive Hughes. *Welsh Division Artillery Prefix 1914–18.*
    k. 1982, Autumn, p. 157, by J.T.M. Reilly. WWI TF Regiment Numbers. Adds to 3e.
    l. Since the last edition, the Order and Medals Research Society must have had many more articles on Regimental Numbers. A further search should reveal more helpful information.
(4) *Identification Data on British War Medals and their Interpretation,* by James R Power, 50pp., NAM and IWM. Short descriptions of numbering system.

(5) *Soldiers Died in the Great War 1914–18,* HMSO, 1921. A copy can be seen on microfilm at PRO, Kew, in the drawer containing the Medal Rolls WO100/...

(6) *The National Roll of the Great War 1914–18,* 14 volumes, National Publishing Company, Very incomplete in its coverage.

(7) *The Medals, Decorations and Orders of the Great War 1914–18,* by A.A. Purves.

4

ARMY DISCHARGE PAPERS 1901–1913
Public Record Office, Kew WO97/5139 et seq.

The long sequence of soldiers' discharge papers in the PRO has recently been extended by the transfer from Army Records of a batch covering the period 1901–13. Although many documents were damaged by fire in 1940, it appears that this series escaped intact. By definition, the soldier had to be discharged at the completion of his service and 'service' includes an appropriate period in the reserves. Should he be recalled to active service, either during his period with the reserves or even after a number of years in civilian life, his documents were retained in or returned to the active file. This means that the papers of a man who was recalled to the Army in 1914 at the outbreak of war, even after his being discharged in, say, 1910, are still retained by Army Records. As a consequence of this recall, which allowed soldiers to re-enlist even up to the age of 55 years if they were skilled craftsmen, e.g. Saddlers or Artificers, most of the 1901–13 batch are for elderly men. Moreover, virtually none of them served in the Great War. This series has thus very little interest to the readers of this book but, as a matter of general interest, it can be stated that they are filed in strict alphabetical order irrespective of regiment or corps. The quantity of names is similar in size to that contained in one quarter's books tn The Family Records Centre, Myddelton Place with the associated problems of selecting the right card from several identical names. It has been found that, on some occasions, men who served before 1914 and had been discharged before that date only to be recalled at the start of the war, have had their papers mis-filed back into the 1901–13 batch if they had been discharged, for a second time, during the war, perhaps on medical grounds. For this reason it is wise to check the 1901–13 batch for all those who received the Silver Badge (see entry on Medal Roll Index Card and Section 12 (sub-section on Wound Stripes and Silver Badge).

All documents for men discharged after 1914, except as mentioned above, are still with the Ministry of Defence and a large proportion were destroyed by bombing in 1940. The remaimng records are now being flmed and will be available in about 1998–2000. They have been allocated the Class Nos. WO363/... and WO364/...

5

LETTERS AND POSTCARDS

Examination of any postcards and envelopes can be rewarding.

Censorship regulations prohibited the mention of the men's location in correspondence so, in theory there should be very few clues in any of the messages. It was not unknown for men to use a simple code to convey messages and location to their loved ones, so a careful study of the text may be revealing. A book on the Duff Cooper family mentions his letters from the Western Front during the war. He apparently had little respect for the censors' knowledge of Shakespeare when he reminded his wife where Polonius met his death*, thus informing her that he was at Arras. In the case of picture postcards, look at the view. It may give a clue. The author's father sent a view showing a picture of the Hanging Virgin of Albert, a very well known landmark. At the time of posting he was only 5 miles from Albert. One does not send a picture of Blackpool Tower when on holiday in Brighton. Another even more obvious clue would be the Regimental Crest. Unit Christmas cards were quite common. Even if the town name has been obscured by the censor, as was quite often done, the card and hence the place can be found in a standard reference book of 1914–18 postcards (Bibl. ref. 1) or from collections in the Imperial War Museum (IWM).

Far less obvious, but very useful, are the postmarks and censor stamps. These can now be decoded to identify the writer's unit with some precision. Unfortunately, many correspondents put postcards into envelopes and these have now been lost. To understand the significance of the marks, one must have some knowledge of the method of transporting mail from France or, for that matter, any other war zone.

After writing his card or letter, the soldier handed his mail into his unit's 'office' unsealed. Here it was read by the unit censor, usually one of the 2nd Lieutenants on a rota basis, impressed with the unit's censor stamp and sealed. During the day the unit's Post Clerk, usually a member of the unit whose duties might be to assist generally in the unit HQ, would take the mail to the Brigade's Field Post Office. This was almost certainly within two or three miles of the soldier's unit. Here, a man from the Royal Engineers Army Postal Service would take the mail from the Post Clerk and hand out any incoming mail for the unit from England. Once at the FPO, the mail would be postmarked with the date-stamped cancellation of that particular FPO. With the daily departure of the motorised Supply Column, the mail, via Divisional HQ, was sent further back to the Division Rail Head and handed over to

---

*Hamlet, Act III, Scene IV.

Fig. 1. A Field Post Office in October 1914. Each FPO had its own rubber date stamp with its own unique number. This can identify its place of posting. The sharp edged, flat topped caps are typical of the early days of the war. Imperial War Museum Q 53350.

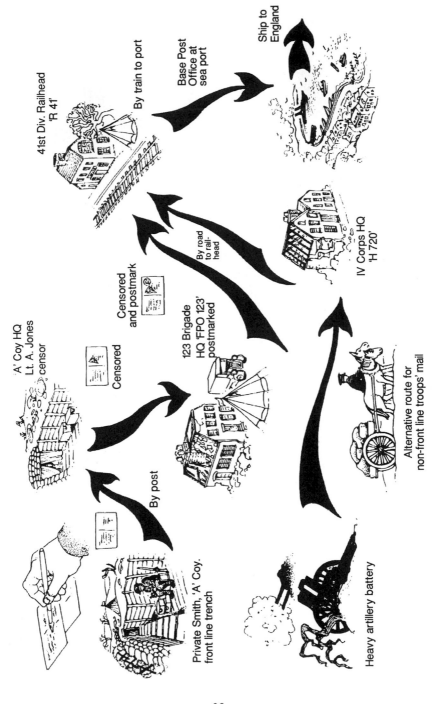

Fig. 2. Diagrammatic arrangement of Army Postal Services in France.

Ship to England

Base Post Office at sea port

41st Div. Railhead 'R 41'

By train to port

Censored and postmark

123 Brigade HQ 'FPO 123' postmarked

By road to rail-head

IV Corps HQ 'H 720'

'A' Coy HQ Lt. A. Jones censor

Censored

By post

Alternative route for non-front line troops' mail

Private Smith, 'A' Coy. front line trench

Heavy artillery battery

Fig. 3. A typical picture postcard. It was No. 157 of a series but the rest of the title has been erased by the censor. The printer's name has been crossed out but is still readable as E. Vignault of Chateau du Loir, a village on a tributary of the River Loire between Le Mans and Tours, SW of Paris.

Fig. 4. The reverse of Fig. 3. Posted on 12th October 1917 at Army Post Office S85 and passed by a Censor with the stamp '5252'. The soldier dates his card '10th October' and states, that we are leaving here for another long journey. The recipient has marked the card 'Received October 16th'. Where was the writer going? The postmark gives a clue. S85 was the stamp of a transit camp at St. Germain au Mont d'Or in the suburbs of Lyon. Had he written his card at his old billet and had to wait until his train stopped at Lyon to post it? At this point of the war our troops were going to North Italy but a search of War Diaries and Orders of Battle should identify the unit.

the Rail Head Army Post Office (see Fig. 1). This was a small sorting office dealing with the mail for several Divisions staffed by four men of the Army Postal Service. From there, the letter would be sent back to the Channel Ports to be shipped to London where it would be delivered to its destination by the normal civilian postal service. Delivery times were two to three days under normal times but during the rapid retreat in the face of the German attack in March 1918, it rose to 10 or more days. For units well back from the front line, extra Army Post Offices provided inputs to the system, each with its own postmark stamp (see Fig. 2). These rubber stamps used by the various types of Army Postal Units are of great interest to the researcher; each had its own unique code number. The same applies to the censor stamp held by every unit of the Army. The records for the allocation of these stamps have long since been lost, but postal history experts have, in most cases, been able to determine the post stamp used by each post office. The simplicity of the system brought fears that the Germans might have been able to break the code, so every six months each office swapped stamps with its neighbours. This exchange arrangement is now fully understood, so knowing the postmark and its date, which of course every stamp carries, the Post Office using it can now be identified. Using the normal Orders of Battle (PRO, Kew or Becke) one can identify the ancestor's unit with a high degree of certainty. Some postmarks from Stationary Offices using 'S' prefixes are still a problem area, as the allocation of these has still not been finally resolved. The key to all these marks is contained in two books on Postal History (Bibl. refs. 2 and 3). The same two books give a little help with Censor marks but here the extent of our knowledge is such that little is known for the period after 1916 and hence the researcher may not be able to interpret the meaning of the number which was unique to the sender's unit. Research on this aspect of WWI is still in progress and anyone unable to solve the mystery of his ancestor's war service should contact the experts in this field for the latest information (Bibl. ref. 4).

The mail was so efficient that the troops would send their washing home! One young officer of the Royal Engineers records in his memoirs that he packed up some surplus clothing into an army sandbag and sent it home. A few days later his mother wrote acknowledging the parcel and returning the sandbag neatly washed and ironed. Her son was able to inform her that this was not necessary as he was in charge of a stores containing some 60,000 bags and these were issued at a rate of 6,000 per day!

Bibliography

(1) *Till the Boys Come Home,* by Toni and Valmai Holt, Macdonald and Janes, 1977.
(2) *History of British Army Postal Service 1903–27,* by E.B. Proud, Proud–Bailey Co. Ltd, Dereham, Norfolk.
(3) *The Postal History of the British Army in World War I,* Before and after 1903–29, by Alistair Kennedy and George Crabb, George Crabb, Epsom 1977.
(4) *Bedfordshire FHS Journal,* Vol. 4, No. 1, Spring 1983.

6

THE BANTAMS

When recruiting started for the 'new armies' in 1914, the minimum height was 5ft 3in. These volunteers were to be formed into 'Service' Battalions. So many men under the height standard came forward that a number of battalions of small men were formed and these became known as 'Bantam Battalions'. The height was supposed to be 5ft 3ins and with at least a 34 inch chest but there is photographic evidence that some men were even smaller. The Surrey Recruiting Registers list several men under 5ft 3ins. One is entered as being 4ft 11ins tall.

At one time the 35th Division, and to a lesser extent the 40th Division, were made up of Bantam Battalions. Some units took the name 'Bantam' which was incorporated into the battalion title. Many used only the normal method of numbering. The men, however, still referred to the fact they were in the Bantams. For those with such family traditions, a list of battalions is given below.

16th Cheshires
15th Cheshires (1st Birkenhead) BBB Bigland's Birkenhead Bamtams (after Alfred Bigland MP)
18th Highland Light Infantry
17th Lancashire Fusiliers
18th Lancashire Fusiliers
20th Lancashire Fusiliers
23rd Manchester Regiment (8th City)
14th Gloucestershire Regiment (West of England Bantams)
15th Sherwood Foresters (Green Diamond Flash on rear of collar)
17th Royal Scots (Lothian Regiment)
19th Durham Light Infantry
19th Royal Welsh Fusiliers
12th South Wales Borderers
17th Welsh Regiment (1st Glamorgan) — 'Rhondda Bantams'
18th Welsh Regiment (2nd Glamorgan)
11th Kings Own Yorkshire Light Infantry (part bantam)
13th Cameronians (Scottish Rifles)
12th Suffolk Regiment
12th South Lancashire Regiment
13th Green Howards — Alexandra Princess of Wales' Own (Yorkshire Regiment)

20th Middlesex Regiment (part bantam)
21st Middlesex Reglment (part bantam)
22nd Middlesex Regiment (part bantam)

Bibliography

The Bantams, by Sidney Allinson, Howard Baker, London, 1981.

7

REGIMENTAL AND BATTALION NAMES

Most researchers will be familiar with the names given to army regiments. The name is usually indicative of the county containing the Regimental Home HQ and/or base. These were often abbreviated for sake of avoiding long names. Hence the Oxfordshire and Buckinghamshire Light Infantry is invariably shortened to the Ox and Bucks. Some regiments are known by less obvious names. The Buffs and Green Howards are but two examples. Other soldiers' nicknames abound, often in questionable taste, but these are not the sort of name that would have been handed down as granddad's old regiment.

The rapid proliferation of battalions within the regiments during the war led to some of the numbered battalions adopting names, both official and unofficial. The private soldier would often refer to these Battalion names. The following is a list brought to the author's attention but it is unlikely to be complete.

A list of the official locally raised battalions given in Army Council Instructions, ACI 228, 3rd December 1914, gives 66 'Pals' battalions with details of founding. Others were added in ACI 172, January 1915. It is reported that 142 battalions were locally raised plus about 62 local Reserve Battalions

Sheffield City Battalion	12th Yorks and Lancashire Regiment
Hallamshire	4th Yorks and Lancashire Regiment
1st and 2nd Barnsley	14th Lancashire Regiment
Wearside Battalion	20th Durham Light Infantry
3rd County Pioneer	22nd Durham Light Infantry
1st and 2nd City of Glasgow	5th and 6th Highland Light Infantry
Blythwood Battalion	7th Highland Light Infantry
Lanark Battalion	8th Highland Light Infantry
Glasgow Highland	9th Highland Light Infantry
1st Glasgow (Tramways)	15th Highland Light Infantry
2nd Glasgow (Boys Brigade)	16th Highland Light Infantry
3rd Glasgow (Chamber of Commerce)	17th Highland Light Infantry
4th Glasgow (Bantam)	18th Highland Light Infantry
Ross Highland	4th Seaforth Highlanders
Sutherland and Caithness Highlanders	5th Seaforth Highlanders
Murrayshire	6th Seaforth Highlanders
Buchan and Formartine	5th Gordon Highlanders

The Shetland Coys	5th Gordon Highlanders
Banff and Donside	6th Gordon Highlanders
Deeside	7th Gordon Highlanders
Lovat Scouts	10th Queen's Own Cameronians
East Belfast	8th Royal Irish
West Belfast	9th Royal Irish
South Belfast	10th Royal Irish
South Antrim	11th Royal Irish
Central Antrim	12th Royal Irish
1st and 2nd County Down	13th, 16th Royal Irish
Young Citizens	14th Royal Irish
North Belfast	15th Royal Irish
County Armagh	9th Royal Irish Fusiliers
1st and 2nd Renfrewshire	5th, 6th Argyll and Sutherland
Argyllshire	8th Argyll and Sutherland
Dumbartonshire	9th Argyll and Sutherland
St. Pancras	16th Rifle Brigade
Western	19th Rifle Brigade
Northern	20th Rifle Brigade
Midland	21st Rifle Brigade
Wessex and Welsh	22nd Rifle Brigade
North Western	23rd Rifle Brigade
Home Counties	24th Rifle Brigade
1st, 2nd Bradford Pals	16th, 18th Prince of Wales's Own West Yorks
	21st Prince of Wales's Own West Yorks
Wool Textile Pioneers	10th, 11th, 12th, 13th East Yorks
1st, 2nd, 3rd, 4th Hull Battalions	
Hull Commercials, Tradesmen's,	
Sportsmen and T'Others)	
South Irish Horse	7th Royal Irish Regiment
1st, 2nd, 4th Salford	15th, 16th, 20th Lancashire Fusiliers
1st, 2nd S.E. Lancs	17th, 18th Lancashire Fusiliers
3rd Salford Pioneers	19th Lancashire Fusiliers
Earl of Chesters	5th Cheshire Regiment
1st, 2nd Birkenhead	15th, 16th Cheshire Regiment
Denbighshire	4th Royal Welsh
Flintshire	5th Royal Welsh
Caernarvonshire and Anglesey	6th Royal Welsh
Merioneth and Montgomery	7th Royal Welsh
1st, 2nd North Wales	13th and 16th Royal Welsh
1st London Welsh	15th Royal Welsh

1st, 2nd, 3rd Brecknockshire	South Wales Borderers
1st, 2nd, 3rd Gwent	10th, 11th, 12th South Wales Borderers
Border Battalions	The King's Own Scottish Borderers
Dumfries and Galloway	5th King's Own Scottish Borderers
County Tyrone	9th Royal Inniskillin
County Derry	10th Royal Inniskillin
County Donegal and Armagh	11th Royal Inniskillin
Bristol	12th Gloucestershire
City of Bristol	4th Gloucestershire
Forest of Dean	13th Gloucestershire
West of England	14th Gloucestershire
Cheltenham	9th Gloucestershire
Church Lads Brigade	16th King's Royal Rifle Corps
British Empire League	17th King's Royal Rifle Corps
British Empire League Pioneers	20th King's Royal Rifle Corps
Arts and Crafts	18th King's Royal Rifle Corps
Yeoman Rifles	21st King's Royal Rifle Corps
Ardwick	8th Manchester Regiment
1st–8th City (of Manchester) (Manchester 'Clerks and Warehousemen')	16th–23rd Manchester Regiment
Oldham Pioneers	24th Manchester Regiment
Scottish (Liverpool Scottish)	9th, 10th King's Liverpool
1st, 2nd, 3rd, 4th City of Liverpool	17th, 18th, 19th, 20th King's Liverpool
Accrington Battalion	11th East Lancs
Bermondsey	12th East Surrey
Wandsworth	13th East Surrey
Cumberland and Westmorland	4th The Border Regiment
Cumberland	5th The Border Regiment
Lonsdale Battalion	11th The Border Regiment
Cinque Ports Battalion	5th Royal Sussex
Horsham	4th Royal Sussex
Hastings	5th Royal Sussex
Worthing	6th Royal Sussex
1st, 2nd, 3rd South Down	11th, 12th, 13th Royal Sussex
Isle of Wight Rifles (Princess Beatrice)	8th Hampshire
Duke of Connaught's Own	6th Hampshire
1st, 2nd Portsmouth	14th, 15th Hampshire
1st, 2nd, 3rd Rhondda	10th, 13th, 20th Welsh Regiment
Swansea	14th Welsh Regiment
Carmarthenshire	15th Welsh Regiment

Cardiff City	16th Welsh Regiment
Cardiff City Commercials	11th Welsh Regiment
1st, 2nd Glamorgan	17/18th Welsh Regiment
Glamorgan Pioneers	19th Welsh Regiment
Welsh Pioneers	23rd Welsh Regiment
Buckinghamshire Battalion	1st Oxford and Buckinghamshire L.I.
Robin Hood	7th Sherwood Forest
Nottingham	15th Sherwood Forest
Chatsworth Rifles	16th Sherwood Forest
Welbeck Rangers	17th Sherwood Forest
Kent County	10th Royal West Kents West
Lewisham	11th Royal West Kents West
Miners Pioneers (Halifax Pals)	12th King's Own Yorkshire L.I.
Public Schools	16th Middlesex Regiment
1st, 2nd Football	17th, 23rd Middlesex Regiment
1st, 2nd, 3rd Public Works Pioneers	8th, 19th, 26th Middlesex Regiment
Shoreditch	20th Middlesex Regiment
Bantam	22nd Middlesex Regiment
Islington	21st Middlesex Regiment
Leeds Rifles	7th, 8th Prince of Wales's Own West Yorks
1st, 2nd Leeds	15th, 17th Prince of Wales's Own West Yorks
City of London Royal Fusiliers	1st—4th Battalion London Regiment
City of London Rifle Brigade	5th Battalion London Regiment
City of London, London Rifles	6th Battalion London Regiment
City of London Post Office Rifles	8th Battalion London Regiment
County of London Queen Victoria's	9th Battalion London Regiment
County of London Hackney Rifles	10th Battalion London Regiment
County of London Finsbury Rifles	11th Battalion London Regiment
County of London The Rangers	12th Battalion London Regiment
Princess Louise's Kensington	13th Battalion London Regiment
County of London, London Scottish	14th Battalion London Regiment
County of London Prince of Wales's Own Civil Service Rifles	15th Battalion London Regiment
County of London Queen's Westminster Rifles	16th Battalion London Regiment
County of London Poplar and Stepney Rifles	17th Battalion London Regiment
County of London, London Irish Rifles	18th Battalion London Regiment
County of London St Pancras	19th Battalion London Regiment

County of London Black Heath and Woolwich	20th Battalion London Regiment
County of London 1st Surrey Rifles	21st Battalion London Regiment
County of London The Queen's	22nd and 24th Battalion London Regt.
County of London The Cyclist	25th Battalion London Regiment
Count of London The Artists Rifles	28th Battalion London Regiment
North Eastern Railway Pioneers	17th Northumberland Fustliers
Tyneside Pioneers	18th–19th Northumberland Fusiliers
Tyneside Scottish	20th, 21st, 22nd, 23rd, 28th, 29th, 33rd Bns.Northumberland Fusiliers
Tyneside Irish	24th/25th, 26th, 27th, 30th, 34th Bns. Northumberland Fusiliers
1st, 2nd, 3rd Birmingham (B'ham Pals)	14th, 15th, 16th Royal Warwickshire
Empire	17th Royal Fusiliers
1st, 2nd, 3rd, 4th Public Schools	18th, 19th, 20th, 21st Royal Fusiliers
Kensington Battalion	22nd Royal Fusiliers
1st, 2nd Sportsman	23rd, 24th Royal Fusiliers
Frontiersmen	25th Royal Fusiliers
Bankers	26th Royal Fusiliers
Jewish Battalion	38th, 39th, 40th, 41st, 42nd, 43rd Royal Fusiliers
East Ham	32nd Royal Fusiliers
Isle of Man	16th King's (Liverpool)
Territorial Rifles	5th, 6th King's (Liverpool)
Irish Battalion (Liverpool Irish)	8th King's (Liverpool)
Durham Pals	18th Durham Light Infantry
Grimsby Chums	10th Battalion Lincolnshire Regiment
Queen's Edinburgh Rifles	4th/5th The Royal Scots
Battersea	10th Royal West Surrey (The Queens)
Lambeth	11th Royal West Surrey (The Queens)
Weald of Kent	5th East Kent (The Buffs)
Cambridgeshire	11th, 13th Suffolk
East Anglian	12th Suffolk
Midland Pioneers	11th Leicestershire Regiment
Tee Side Pioneers	12th Alexandra Princess of Wales's Own (Yorkshire Regiment)
Severn Garrison	4th Lancashire Fusiliers
Humber Garrison	3rd Lancashire Fusiliers
Severn Valley Pioneers	4th Worcestershire
Cornwall Pioneers	10th Duke of Cornwall's Light Infantry
St Helens	11th Prince of Wales's (South Lincs)

City of Dundee	4th Black Watch (Royal Highlanders)
Angus and Dundee	5th Black Watch (Royal Highlanders)
Perthshire	6th Black Watch (Royal Highlanders)
Fife	7th Black Watch (Royal Highlanders)
West Ham	13th Essex Regiment
Green Cross Corps	Women's Reserve Ambulance Corps

Bibliography

Locally Raised Units, Lists of Units raised by Communities, etc., War Office, London, August 1916.

8

ELECTORAL ROLLS

One particularly valuable source of information on a soldier's unit is the Absent Voters List. It is a source that is often overlooked, but one that gives more information than most.

An Act of Parliament passed on 6th February 1918 allowed service men to register in order to obtain a vote in the constituency of their home address. The first lists were published on the 15th October 1918 from applications received up to the 18th August 1918. The second appeared on 15th April 1919 for applications up to 18th February 1919. (There may have been an earlier issue but due to the short notice after the passing of the Act most men would not have had time to register.) Although the arrangement continued for some time at the same six monthly intervals, the subsequent issues are not nearly as important as many men were now back at home but it is always as well to check.

The lists were prepared by the local Electoral Officer who had to publish them in the same manner as the normal voters lists, twice a year. They appeared as completely separate books from the ordinary lists, each covering the whole or part of a constituency and entitled *Absent Voters Lists* (see Fig. 6). The information was given by the soldier, not by his dependants, *and would be that applying just before the appropriate qualifying date* (18th February or 18th August) (see Fig. 5). It is usual to give, in addition to the home address, the following information: surname Christian names, regiment or corps, regimental number, rank, battalion, battery (for artillery units), company or other unit number (for other corps units). There appears to have been no set standard entry and some men added details such as 'attached to Egyptian Army' or 'East Africa'. The lists for each constituency are arranged by town or village, by streets in street number order. All odd numbers of a street were preceded by even numbers so that, in long streets No. 2 was on a different page from No. 1. In other areas, the names were arranged in alphabeticai order of surname. The address was the one that would have given the soldier a vote had he not been in the forces. This would normally be the man's home address. Voters lists can be found at the local library, Town Hall or the CRO. The whereabouts of a complete set is not known; the British Library's collection for the period of the war is very limited. Bear in mind that it is the Absent Voters' list that is required. There was also a list of men having Proxy votes reported to give the service address of the men and those entitled to vote for them. The whereabouts of these Proxy lists is not known but they are believed to concern men serving overseas other than in France. It cannot be stated too often that the information given refers to the soldier's unit number, etc. at the

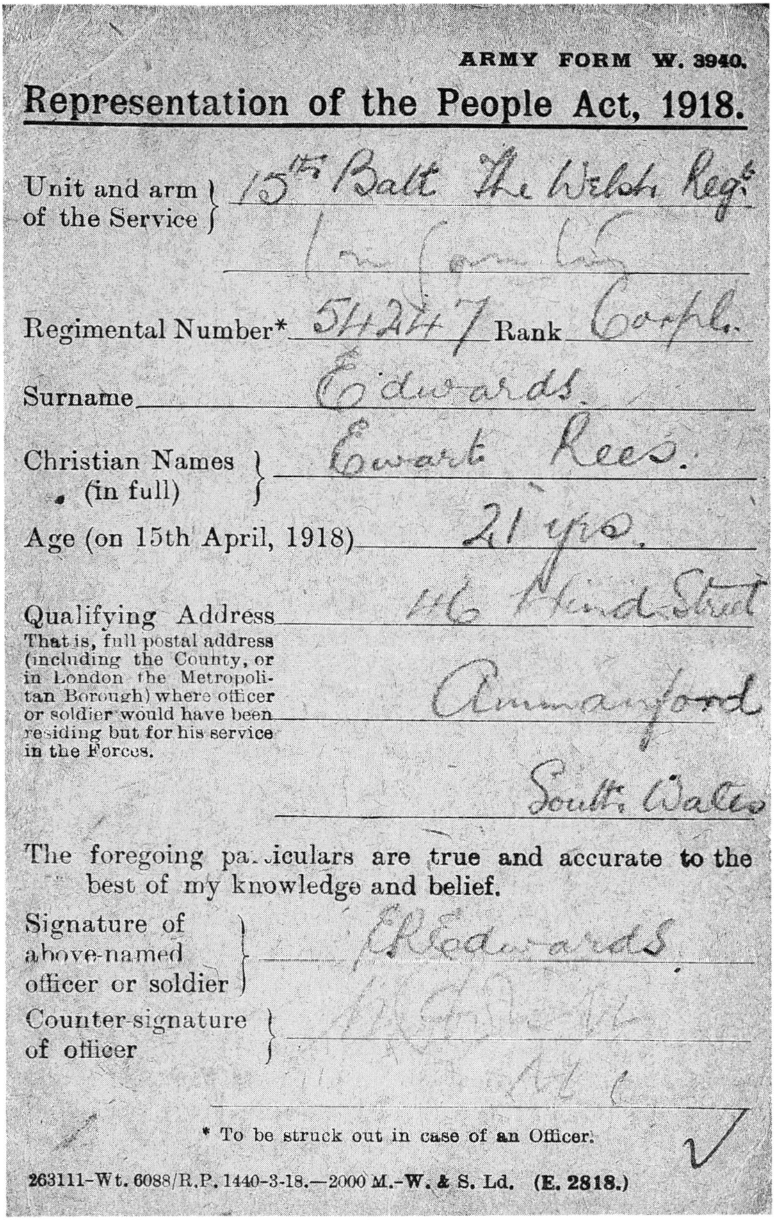

Representation of the People Act, 1918.

Unit and arm of the Service } *15ᵗʰ Batt The Welsh Regᵗ*

I m Comm Ly

Regimental Number* *54247* Rank *Corpl.*

Surname *Edwards.*

Christian Names (in full) } *Ewart Rees.*

Age (on 15th April, 1918) *21 yrs.*

Qualifying Address *116 Hind Street*

That is, full postal address (including the County, or in London the Metropolitan Borough) where officer or soldier would have been residing but for his service in the Forces.

Ammanford

South Wales

The foregoing particulars are true and accurate to the best of my knowledge and belief.

Signature of above-named officer or soldier } *E R Edwards.*

Counter-signature of officer }

* To be struck out in case of an Officer.

263111-Wt. 6088/R.P. 1440-3-18.—2000 M.-W. & S. Ld. (E. 2818.)

Fig. 5. The official postcard used by a soldier to inform the Registration Officer in his home town of his wish to be registered as an Absent Voter. He had to be over 19.

50

ABSENT VOTERS' LIST.

PARLIAMENTARY COUNTY OF BEDFORD.

BEDFORD DIVISION.

POLLING DISTRICT A.

PARISH OF ST. CUTHBERT, BEDFORD.

	Names in full. (Surname first.)	Qualifying Premises.	Description of Service. Ship, Regiment, Number, Rank, Rating, &c., or recorded address.	5 No.
	Electoral Division 8.			
1	Macleod, Bannatyne	Goldington Road	164826 2 Pte., R.A.F.	1
2	Owen, Alfred Walter	13 St. Cuthbert's Sq.	154854 Pte., D Co. East. Com. Labour Centre	2
3	Cooper, William Henry	6 St. Cuthbert s St.	49078 Spr., 1/6 Cyc. Bn. S'f'k.	3
4	Stanton, Geoffrey J. G.	Goldington Road	55190 Pte., 1st Manchester	4
5	Cave, Thomas	Goldington Road	H/231607 Pte., 1/1st Dorset Y.	5
6	Porter, Thomas Brandon	38 Mill Street	768099 Pte., 2 Artists' Rifles O.T.C.	6
7	Dickins, Joseph Mark	12 St. Cuthbert's Sq.	201342 Pte., 1/4th Norfolks	7
8	Fenn, James Mills	8 St. Cuthbert's St.	S/4125635 Pte., 2/3rd Field Bakery, A.S.C.	8
	Electoral Division 9. BOWER STREET.			
9	Morris, Harry James	27	43093 a/Sgt., 13 Sig. Co. R.E.	9
10	Johnson, Frank	41	33644 Pte., 3rd Beds (P of W)	10
11	Croshaw, William Alfred	53	224488 Spr., 232 A.T.C., R.E.	11
12	Bryant, Thomas Arthur	57	20355 Gnr., R.G.A.	12
13	Carter, Harry	61	128002 R.A.M.C.	13
14	Hawkes, Richard	67	395727 L/C., 482 Agl. Lab. Co	14
15	Freshwater, Ernest Wm.	85	F/244629 A.C.2, R.A.F.	15

Fig. 6. Part of the Absent Voters' List prepared from information supplied by the soldier. Note the precise details of the soldier's unit.

time he completed his form and this could change frequently, particularly after the Armistice on 11th November 1918 when many units were disbanded and men transferred to others.

There is another interesting list from the war period as the result of the 1915 National Registration Act. This was a virtual census of all adults, complete with occupations, made to evaluate the available manpower. These lists were compiled locally and were made available to Electoral Officers. However, most appear to have been lost. It has been reported that the Yeovil list was found on a rubbish tip and is now preserved. If one has survived, so may others, so it is worth enquiring at you local library, Town Hall or CRO. However, the survey of sources has failed to locate a single example of this list. Details of the organisation are given in WO/62/6 pp. 71 and 72 (PR0, Kew).

Where a soldier was stationed at a UK camp for a longish period, he could register his vote in the normal manner. His name would appear in the normal Voters' List. No military rank or number was stated, but the finding of the ancestor's name in the list for a camp would prove that he had, in fact, been stationed there as a member of the permanent staff.

9

MILITARY MUSEUMS

In theory, almost every one of the WWI Regiments has a museum covering its activities during the war (Bibl. refs. 1–4). In practice, it is something very different. Often the display is a few medals and a walking out uniform in a glass show case in a corner of a town museum. Others are housed in the Regimental HQ of the modern successor to the old regiment. In the first case, there are usually no documents at all although these may have been passed to the local CRO for safekeeping. Alternatively, they may still be with a retired officer of the regiment to whom enquiries are passed. In the second case, the records are housed in a small shelf-lined room with one searcher's chair and desk. The index is very scanty and the only archivist is the Curator who also acts as Regimental Secretary, Secretary to the Regimental Association, Editor of the Regimental Journal and, in some cases, the officer in command of the Home HQ of the Regiment. The post usually carries the rank of Lieutenant-Colonel (ret'd) but it can be held by a civilian and a knowledge of or interest in the history of the regiment is not always a requirement for the job. In addition to the duties listed above, one curator explained the delay in replying to a letter by saying that he had been seconded to help arrange the Royal Tournament at Wembley. Many military museums are very short of money and many have, in fact, closed.

For these reasons, only a very few regiments are prepared to carry out searches even of the most elementary kind and even the acknowledgement of a letter may take weeks. On the other hand, most are prepared to allow the researcher to examine their records by appointment. Usually the only person who knows anything about the records is the curator himself and as he has so many other responsibilities he may not always be available, and you will find yourself there with only his assistant who knows even less about the records. Therefore, at least for the first visit, make sure the curator will be available.

The first visit to one of the larger museums to carry out research is an interesting experience. On approaching the entrance you are ushered past the turnstile and directed upstairs to the Colonel's office. The Colonel is usually seated behind a vast leather-covered desk at the far end of a cavernous room which would do justice to a film set for a German General in his HQ (British Generals always seem to use Nissen Huts!). Nowadays, the khaki uniform has been replaced by a Harris tweed jacket and cavalry twill trousers but the military bearing remains. After a few pleasant words of greeting you are ushered along the corridor to the archives. No search room and a long wait for documents; just a small desk with a wooden chair set between the storage shelves. A few brief comments about the index system, a few words of advice and you are on your own. Don't forget to ask about lunch — you might get locked in!

Do not expect to make rapid progress, as in most museums the indexes are rudimentary and few lists of names are extant. Be prepared to have to search through volumes of orders, printed books and albums of photographs.

Apart from the very rare Nominal Rolls the things to look for are Regimental and Battalion Orders, Press Cuttings, Photographs, histories and plans of Campaigns and Depots. Always, if possible, check the printed histories before visiting the museum so that you know at least a little about the history of the regiment or corps and the names and origins of the numerous battalions. The bookshelf should contain a full set of the printed histories, including some that may not be generally available. There may also be a few private diaries. If any of the histories are of recent publication, check if the author is still alive, as he is probably the 'Regiment's Historian', a real gold mine of information if you can contact him, and like most enthusiasts, only too pleased to talk about his pet subject. Don't give up the search if the Nominal Roll you had hoped to find does not exist. Regimental Oders may give details of the ancestor's promotion to Corporal. A few pencilled notes may recall details of a bulk transfer of men from one battalion to another at a date or place which matches Family Tradition. The photograph album may show the cross country team of the 6th Battalion who beat the 7th Battalion on the 6th December 1915 and there in the back row is grandfather in his long shorts. The possibilities are endless, but the chances of a direct mention of the ancestor are slim.

A questionnaire has been sent to all known Military Museums. Replies were received from about 85% and these have been used to compile the lists in Bibl. ref. 5. In most cases, the replies reveal the printed books on the regiment, a few Nominal Rolls and Regimental Orders. This does not mean that it is not worthwhile writing to the Museum as they often have collections of photographs, etc. as mentioned above. More and more military museums are trying to compile indexes of all men that served in their regiments. Because of the lack of records these are made up from names extracted from many sources, including newspapers, rolls of honour, etc. (Essex, Gloucestershire, and Oxfordshire and Buckinghamshire).

Bibliography

(1) *A Guide to Military Museums,* compiled by Terence Wise, Athena Books, 20 St. Marys Road, Doncaster DNI 2NP, 1986.

(2) *Britain's Regimental Museums,* by Roy Batten, 199 Chiswick Village, London W4 3DG.

(3) Army Museums Ogilby Trust, Connaught Barracks, Duke of Connaught's Road, Aldershot, Hants. GU11 2LR. This acts as a co-ordinator for all Military Museums and may be able to advise on the records of specific regiments not mentioned in Bibl. refs.1 and 2.

(4) The National Army Museum has a file on the records held by the principal Military Museums.

(5) *The Location of British Army Records 1914–18,* by Norman Holding, 3rd edn., Federation of Family History Societies.

10

MEDICAL RECORDS

One of the longest lists of men who survived the war that is available to the public is to be found in the medical records at the PRO, Kew, class MH106/. . . It comprises some two thousand boxes, but is of limited use as it contains only a sample of the original records and it is very inadequately indexed.

During the war every treatment point for wounded or sick men had an Admissions Book in which the name, initials, rank, number, regiment or corps, platoon, company or other unit together with the date of admission was entered. There was also a brief mention of the reason for admission, often a set of initials and the date of discharge or transfer. The importance of the entry to the family historian is the exact denomination of the casualty's unit, albeit in bad handwriting.

The method of dealing with casualties was complex but effective and was not changed extensively during the course of the war except for the introduction of the Motor Ambulance Convoy in November 1914 and issuing of motor ambulance cars to Field Ambulances at the same time. The wounded man was helped or carried by his comrades to the Regimental Aid Post; this was just one doctor of the Royal Army Medical Corps assisted by approximately 32 private soldiers of the regiment, acting as stretcher bearers — they were usually members of the Regimental Band. The Aid Post would be 'housed' in a shell hole or trench a few yards behind the front line. At this point, a label would be tied to the patient and a tear-off part of this label would be retained by the Regimental Aid Post staff. Both parts would give details of the wound, name, rank, number, etc. (see Fig. 7). The treatment would be limited to a field dressing and an injection with morphia. The patient would then be taken back to the Advanced Dressing Station. This would be about two to five miles behind the front line and transport would depend on the type. or severity of the wound, the choice available being walking, sitting in a lorry, sitting in an ambulance car (in the early days in a horse ambulance), carried by stretcher either on foot, by ambulance or on a special miniature railway.

At the A.D.S. some attempt could be made to treat the wound but in most cases only the dressing was changed. Upon entering the Dressing Station, the patients' numbers were taken and entered in the Admissions Book. Men reporting sick were also dealt with. Assuming the wound was bad enough to prevent return to duty after simple treatment, the patient would await his turn in the queue for a place in one of the string of motor ambulances of the Motor Ambulance Convoy, to take him to the next point of treatment, the Casualty Clearing Station. When the pressure of battle gave rise to a large number of casualties, the ambulant patients would be conveyed by lorry and a number of extra Collecting Stations were set up (see Fig. 8).

Fig. 7. Stretchers Bearers at the Battle of the Menin Bridge, Potijze, 20th September 1917 make the first record of the personal details of a wounded soldier. A few sets of similar details survive in the series of Medical Unit Admission Books in the PRO at Kew; MHI06/... (IWM Q285l).

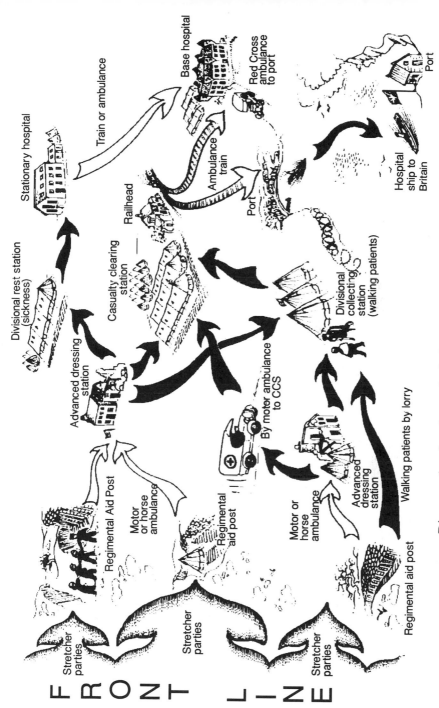

Diagram showing the method of transportation of casualities.

The Casualty Clearing Stations were very large tented hospitals, each with up to 800 beds usually arranged in groups of three or four in the neighbourhood of a railway siding. This enabled patients to be easily loaded on to waiting ambulance trains. Each of the Casualty Clearing Stations within the group would admit patients until full. Hence the entries in the Admissions Book, which each kept, would be in large batches of several hundred confined to periods of one or two days or even a few hours followed by no more entries for several days.

The duties of the Casualty Clearing Station were threefold:

(1) to return the patient to the front;
(2) to transfer him to the Base Hospital, usually in England, for complete recovery;
(3) if neither of these was possible due to the severity of the patient's injury or condition, to give sufficient treatment and/or rest to enable him to travel.

Full operating facilities were available and a small staff of female nurses was assisted by members of the Royal Army Medical Corps. Teams of convalescent patients were also employed. All of this in a collection of tents only 7 to 30 miles from the front line, sometimes within range of shell fire and often subject to bombing, in spite of the Red Cross flag flying overhead. Further details of medical services during the war are given in Bibl. ref. 1.

Operations were recorded in a separate Log Book and each patient had a case card, probably kept at the foot of his bed and a record card 'in the office'.

Should the patient be forwarded via ambulance train and hospital ship to England, he would be logged both en route and at the Base Hospital, which was usually near a French sea port, and upon arrival at the hospital in England. The CCS's moved back and forth with the tide of battle and had of necessity to be tented or hutted. Base and Stationary Hospitals were well back from the front line and usually housed in the grounds of a chateau or similar large building. The researcher can thus see that there was plenty of documentation recordmg the travel (and the condition) of the wounded or sick soldier. Even allowing for men who were wounded more than once, the cards probably covered more than half the total army. After the war, all these records came together and appear to have been used for two purposes.

Firstly, a sample of the soldiers' cards giving details of each occurrence of sickness or wounding was extracted and filed into about 50 classes of different illnesses and wounds. The results of this analysis were used to compile a book *Medicnl Statistics* (Bibl. ref. 2). This describes the records in detail. The sample was large, about 50,000 − 100,000, but this represents less than 5% of the total wounded of two and a half million and probably as many cases of sickness. Secondly, the whole of the records were used to verify claims for pensions, etc. due to war wounds. Hence the whole set of records ended up at the Ministry of Health and Pensions. All 126 tons of them! Details of the method of filing and use, prepared for those who had to deal with the files, can be found in Bibl. refs. 3 and 4.

By 1975, all those liable to claim pensions were receiving old age pensions anyway so the records were no longer needed for their original purpose and nearly the whole lot were destroyed. However, a small sample was retained and is now in the PRO, Kew (MH106/. . .) — a total of 2 tons in some 2,000 boxes.

For those with patience and luck, they might reveal some interesting facts. It is believed that the entire statistical sample of the cards in their original categories has been kept: at least there are two sequences of piece numbers each containing some 50 categories, one for illness or disease (e.g. trench foot, VD) and the other group for wounds (foot wounds, head wounds). The cards are arranged in unknown order, and give name, number, rank, unit (regiment or corps, battalion or company) and type of wound or illness. The back has brief details of treatment and condition in doctor's scrawl! There is no index! If you know for a fact that the ancestor had a particular wound, e.g. he had only one leg or a bad scar, then it might be worth a search in the appropriate category on the off chance that his case was selected.

The next group consists of the Admissions Books — sometimes operations were recorded at the end of the same book — for an approximate 5–10% sample of FAs, CCSs, Base Hospitals (France) and Base Hospitals (UK). The books are sometimes indexed by initial letter of the surname but even this limited aid still leaves the researcher with many pages of names to search through for even a short period.

The allocation of Field Ambulances (a unit not a vehicle) to Divisions is given in Table 4 but can also be obtained from Becke or from GHQ Orders of Battle. One can then relate the ancestor's known location on a known date to a Division by using the official history or Becke and hence obtain the Field Ambulances dealing with wounded from that Division for the time in question. A Manual (ref. MH106/2389) gives a list of locations for all Casualty Clearing Stations, Stationary and Base Hospitals in France (see Table 4) but it does not indicate which Field Ambulance sent patients to which CCS. This information can be obtained from the reading of the War Diary of the Motor Ambulance Convoy allocated to that corps at the time in question. It was normal for the Diary to state which FAs were cleared to which CCSs. In quiet times, it was normal to segregate patients according to the wound or sickness so that all self-inflicted wounds, for example, would be sent to one CCS within an Army area and eye injuries to another.

For the move from CCS to Base Hospital, the source of information is not known, but it is likely that the War Diaries of the 30-odd Ambulance trains may be of help. However, with the Admissions Books of only a few hospitals and CCSs extant, it is doubtful whether the complete route of any one soldier can be traced in this manner. War Diaries of General Hospitals near ports often give the name of the hospital ship or other transport by which patients were transferred to England. Names of patients do not appear except for the occasional death.

In general, the books are not worth searchin unless

(a) You know the ancestor was serving with a Division covered by one of the five extant FAs Admission Books. This might trace an entry for the ancestor reporting sick or for treatment of an, up till now, unknown wound.

(b) You know the date of an injury or sickness from a War Diary and/or family sources. It might be worth searching the books for all FAs, CCSs and Hospitals for that date or just after it.

(c) If you know that the ancestor was gassed, then MH106/2386 gives a list of Medical Units known to have handled gas patients, but records of only three survive (see Table 4).

(d) Alternatively, if the ancestor's unit is not known but it is known he was gassed, the list of gas treatment units with the dates given and their locations at that time could provide an additional set of data to be used to identify the unit. In this case, the medical records themselves are not needed, only the list of gas treatment centres (MH106/2386). This list of treatment centres should be complete but there is evidence to show that there were others, so your deductions may be flawed.

If you know the type of gas which afflicted the ancestor then you have another clue which may tie the date down to a narrower period. Chlorine gas was first used on 22nd April 1915. Phosgene came into use on 15th December 1915 and Mustard gas was not introduced until 12th July 1917 but was also used in Salonika. The Admission Books cover 100% of all cases admitted to the few medical units whose records remain. A word of warning — due to the large numbers involved, several men of the same surname and initials could pass through a CCS within a short period. Bear in mind also that the FAs always move with their Division while CCSs were far less mobile and Base Hospitals nearly always stayed in one spot. The Instruction Manual for the records (ref. MH106/2386) gives every location of every CCS, Base and Stationary Hospital and hence is a valuable aid.

The last group of records in Table 4 is the easiest to use. They cover the members of a small number of the multitude of regiments and corps. It is not known if there was a card for every man or woman or even if all the cards have survived in the remaining records. A brief examination of a trial box showed the cards to be in regimental number order. The regiments covered are also given in the table. The term 1st and 2nd Hussars appears in the indexes, but this is an error as there were no such regiments. It could mean the 1st and 2nd Dragoons. Anyone suspecting that they had an ancestor in any one of these regiments should make a point of searching the appropriate box. The cards from the Royal Field Artillery are particularl valuable as they give the Brigade and Battalion of the men, a piece of vital information that is very difficult to find anywhere else. At this point, it would not be out of place to warn the researcher that transfers within the RFA were common and the fact that a man appears in one Brigade on a certain date does not mean he spent the whole war with that unit.

Another set of Medical Records for the pre-war period 1904—14 is in the Cheshire CRO. This contains notification forms for infectious diseases for the NW Military District and contains reports of units to the many camps and depots in the area by the Sanitary Officer. Records include general Corps and Army orders for the period.

Copies of *The War Office Weekly, Casualty Lists* have been found in the National Newspaper Library, Colindale, the Library of Scotland, Edinburgh and perhaps in Manchester Library. These Lists date from 7th August 1917 for casualties reported before 30th July 1917. The whereabouts of earlier issues is not known. They continue until 4th March 1919 and include Air Force casualties after 9th July 1918. They are not indexed.

TABLE 4

List of the medical units whose records remain, together with their locations and dates

General Hospitals

No. 2 General Hospital, Le Havre, France	17 Aug 1914—24 Feb 1919
No. 18 General Hospital, Camiers, France,	26 Apr 1915—28 Jan 1919
also Medical Board Reports	
No. 19 General Hospital, Alexandria, Egypt,	27 Apr 1915—23 Nov 1918
also Medical Board Reports	
No. 28 General Hospital, Salonika,	21 Nov 1915—23 May 1919
also Medical Board Reports	
No. 85 General Hospital Murmansk, Russia	23 Aug 1918—20 Sep 1918
Bakaritza, Russia,	22 Sep 1918—2 Sep 1919
also Medical Board Reports	
No. 4 Stationary Hospital, St Omar 1916	15 Sep 1914-1918
(shell shock 1st and 2nd Armies)	
Arques, France	May 1918—Dec 1918
Longuenesse, 5th Army	Dec 1918—
HM Hospital Ship *Assaye*	30 Jul 1915—Mar 1921
No. 31 Ambulance Train, France	16 Jul 1916—20 Feb 1918
Italy	20 Feb 1918—7 Jul 1918
France	8 Jul 1918—Nov 1918

UK Hospitals — Admissions Books

Napsbury	29 May 1915—Jul 1919
also Medical Sheets	
Queen Alexandra's, Millbrook	Aug 1914—May 1919
also Medical Sheets	
Catterick Military Hospital	Aug 1916—Jan 1919
also Medical Sheets	
Craiglockhart	Oct 1916—Feb 1919
Catterick Command Depot	
also Medical Sheets	

Field Ambulances — Admission Books

14th Field Ambulance
24.08.14	20.11.18	France 5th Div., 20.08.14
(Gas April 1918)		
		Italy 5th Div., 12.12.17
		04.04.18

51st Field Ambulance
| 17.07.15 | 13.08.18 | France 17th Div. |

66th Field Ambulance
| 18.10.15 | 13.10.18 | France 22nd Div., 07.09.15 |
| | | Salonika, 15.11.15 |

139th Field Ambulance
07.05.16	06.09.18	France 41st Div.
(Gas Sept 1918)		04.05.16
		Italy, 17.11.17
		02.03.18

Casualty Clearing Stations

No. 3 CCS
Aug 1914	26.04.15	Hazebrouk
27.04.15	14.05.15	Poperinghe
15.05.15	31.03.16	Bailleul
01.04.16	15.05.16	St. Ouen
16.05.16	06.03.17	Puchevillers
12.03.17	15.04.17	Aveluy
16.04.17	27.03.18	Grenvillers
28.03.18	14.09.18	Gezaincourt
21.09.18	26.10.18	Beaulencourt
02.11.18	05.02.19	Caudry

No. 11 CCS
19.06.16	13.08.16	Doublens Citadel
14.08.16	09.10.16	Gezaincourt
10.10.16	14.05.17	Barennes
28.05.17	15.07.17	Bailleul
16.07.17	15.04.18	Godewaersvelde
16.04.18	28.04.18	Blendecques
29.04.18	06.10.18	Moulte
07.10.18	27.10.18	Brielen
28.10.18	19.03.19	St Anne
20.03.19	May 1919	Steenwerch

No. 31 CCS
EEF

30.10.15	20.11.15	Alexandria, Sidi Bishr

BSF

26.11.15	31.07.16	Salonika, Monastir Road
01.08.16	18.10.18	Janes
22.10.18	Embarked on *Agamemnon* 22.03	Salonika
26.10.18		Dedbagach

No. 34 CCS

31.12.15	03.01.16	Marseilles
03.01.16	29.01.16	Carcassonne
01.02.16	30.04.16	Boulogne
04.05.16	10.05.16	Daours
23.05.16	09.09.16	Vecquemont
09.09.16	15.04.17	Grovetown
16.04.17	01.07.17	Peronne la Chapelette
01.07.17	12.08.17	Tincourt
13.08.17	31.08.17	St Idesbald
01.09.17	21.11.17	Zuydcote
28.11.17	27.12.17	St Omer
28.12.17	23.03.18	Marchelpot
15.04.18	13.06.18	Etaples
13.06.18	31.10.18	Fienvillers
01.11.18	30.12.18	Solesmes

No. 39 CCS
BEF

06.03.16	01.08.16	Etaples
02.05.16	31.07.16	St Ouen
01.08.16	09.02.17	Allonville
11.02.17	03.05.17	Gailly
05.17	30.06.17	Tincourt
01.07.17	09.07.17	Peronne la Chapelette
10.07.17	21.11.17	Oosthoek

Italian Ex. force

26.11.17	01.04.18	Istrana
04.04.18	18.10.18	Montevecchio Villa Buechia (eapo 5otto)
18.10.18	17.11.18	Mirano
18.11.18		Vicenza

No. 82 CCS

Aug 1918	Sept 1919	Russia

Soldiers' Records

Regiments by Regiment Number

Leicester Regiment	16 boxes out of 16 survive
Royal Field Artillery	18 boxes out of 216 survive
Grenadier Guards	11 boxes out of 11 survive
Hussars	6 boxes out of 6 survive
Royal Flying Corps	5 boxes out of 27 survive

Womens' Services

VAD
Hospital
Scots Womens Hospital
Womens' League   } 3 boxes total
WRNS
QMAAS

Statistical Survey

29 boxes of Diseases and Illnesses
22 boxes of Wounds in Regimental Number Order

Bibliography

(1) *Medical History of the War,* by Major-General Sir W.G. MacPherson, 4 volumes. General History. Details movements of RAMC units during the war.
(2) *Casualties and Medical Statistics of the Great War,* by Major T.J. Mitchell and Miss G.M. Smith, 1931, HMSO. Explains the records that still exist in MH106/...
(3) *Manual for Clerks,* MH106/2389.
(4) *Lists of Units and Locations,* MH106/2386.

11

RECRUITING AND OTHER REGISTERS

Many ledgers, books and registers were used during the war to record various aspects of the soldier's life and death. Most of these were destroyed after the war but some survived and are now coming to light. The Surrey CRO at Kingston-on-Thames has a set of 44 bound books of which some 37 cover the war perriod (ref. 2496/1-44).

These 37 books cover at least 100,000 names. No other county reports holding any similar records and there is no information on the purpose of these volumes. The following is deduced after a quick perusal of six sample books and the CRO Catalogue.

The books appear to list all men who enlisted at several recruiting offices from East Surrey. This may be defined as the 31st Regimental District Recruiting Area, which title appears on some of the volumes (Nos. 30, 42, 106). Volume 44 refers to No. 2 Regimental District, Guildford. These numbers refer to the old East Surrey and West Surrey Regimental Depots, respectively. The information given in the books implies that the men had been medically examined and allocated to many differing regiments and corps. All the names are recorded in the Army Book No. 303 *Register of Recruits.* This consists of 200 numbered double pages plus a thumb indexed section at the end which is used in some books only to compile a 'first letter only' index of names. The columns are headed:-

Regiment/ Name/ Initial/ Age (years and months).
Height (feet and inches)/ Chest (inches)/ Weight (pounds).
Colour of complexion/ Eyes/ Hair/ Distinguishing Marks.
Occupation/ Type of Reserve or TF unit if any.
Place of Birth/ Date of Attestation/ Where and by whom.
Name of Recruiter/ Recruiting Agent/ Medical Officer.
If or when Accepted or Rejected and by whom/ Remarks.
This last column appears to have been used to put in home address.

The columns are not always filled in and some are used for purposes other than that given at the head of the column. The 'accepted/rejected' column is usually used to enter the depot to which the recruit is sent for training, e.g. ASC to Grove Park, ROC to Woolwich', etc. Each man has been allocated a number, but this was not the regimental number, just the number of the entry in the book. (AC1232 28th July 1915 states that each recruit must have a Recruiting Office number.) Other books, e.g. No. 44, give the medical grade, i.e. A, B1, B2, B3, etc. (A1, A2, etc. were not introduced until June 1916.) Only A and B could serve in France, C—E were only fit for home duty, at least for the first two years of the war. The regimental number is given in some books, e.g. No. 44, in addition to the book sequence number. These appear to be different from the numbers being issued to other men of that regiment or corps at the same time and hence are rather puzzling. It is known that some depots held blocks of numbers for transfers but the whole field of regimental numbers is most unclear, e.g. in 1917 Book No. 44 allocated numbers of the order of 40,000 to ASC men when the numbers should have been over 200,000 by then.

The books can be grouped into different dates.

The first group, Nos. 35–40 and 1–6, covers the period before the war with the earliest starting in 1908 when the Army was reformed. The period 4 August 1914 to January 1916 (i.e. up to the start of the Derby Scheme) is covered by several books and the difference between them is not clear. What is more, the series runs on past the start of conscription in March 1916 (Nos. 38, 39 and 6). A very large number of men enlisted in the first six months of the war and the numbers of men entered in the books do not appear to be sufficient. Hence it is suspected that some books are missing.

The second batch covers Groups of the Lord Derby Scheme (Nos. 7–14). Derby men registered between 16th October 1915 and 15th December 1915 and were 'called up' in 23 age groups between 15th January 1916 and 13th June 1916. Men had to report for duty a few weeks after their 'call up'. Entries in the books start on 10th January but continue up to December 1916. The last two books, Nos.13 and 14, cover the period between the end of August and December and carry titles 'Groups O' and 'Groups 28' which imply a deviation from the norm, but the precise meaning is not known. Although the books carry titles which include a Group number, e.g. 'Book 3', 'Group 3' (CRO/9), the men listed therein come from all age groups and not just Group 3 who should be single men aged about 20–21 years. Hence the title is misleading. Note also that there are two books titled 'Book 3' (CRO/9 and /13) and no 'Book 5'.

The third set of books covers the period of conscription, i.e. 3rd March 1916 to the end of the war (Books 15–24), but the series appears to end by September 1917. Conscription age categories were called Classes.

There appears to be a number of books which do not fit any of the above series, i.e. Nos. 25–29, 41 and 44. The titles give an indication that they cover special units, i.e. No. 26 (Hon. Artillery Company – an officer training unit) and No. 25 (Royal Ordnance Corps). Other areas, viz. South London Recruiting Area, are covered in Nos. 27–29 and No. 44 covers the 2nd Regimental District. There is some evidence that the term HAC and perhaps ROC refer to a recruiting office and/or district and not to the fact that all recruits were to be sent to these units.

The following towns are mentioned on the covers of the books. These may be recruiting centres.

Croydon	Epsom	Kingston	Mitcham
Peckham	Richmond	R. O. Woolwich	Upper Norwood
Wandsworth	Weybridge	Wimbledon	

VAD 3rd Battalion East Surrey Regiment
VAD Supplementary Reserve
HAC
South London Recruiting

No other Recruiting Registers are known except some in the Museum of the Duke of Cornwall's Light Infantry, Bodmin which has a number of books which run from October 1905 to October 1916 with a few gaps. It is believed that these refer only to the DCLI.

The NAM (Royal Hospital Road, Chelsea, London) now has in its collection a large number of registers concerning money owing in the form of back pay to soldiers who had died in service. These cover the period 1901 to 1960. Unfortunately, the amount of shelf space needed to store the several hundred volumes means that, for many years, they will not all be available for public search. The importance of these registers to family historians is that they give the names and, in some cases, addresses of the next-of-kin to whom the back pay and effects were to be sent. Other information given includes name, rank, Regimental or Army number, date and place of death (may be limited to the words 'France and Flanders' only). Indication is also given of the presence of a Will. The records are fully indexed.

Leaflets describing the records can be obtained from the Head of Department of Archives, Photographs, Film and Sound (self-addressed, stamped envelope or three International Reply Coupons, please). By 1998, those registers dealing with 'other' ranks' who died between 1901 and August 1914 and from 31 March 1921 to 1960 and officers who died in the period 1902–1960 will be available. 'Other ranks' for the period 1914-1921 will probably not be available for many years.

12

PHOTOGRAPHS

Most families with WWI connections have a photograph or two showing the ancestor in uniform. This can be a valuable clue to the researcher but one that is full of pitfalls for the unwary.

Consider the case of a detective working on an important but difficult case. His chief clue is a photograph showing a group of Morris Dancers on a lawn with a large church in the background. It would be of great help to him if he could identify the place, the date it was taken and the names of the dancers. His first action was to show the photograph to an expert on church architecture. At once it was identified as St. Albans Cathedral. A phone call to the Dean located the leader of a group of dancers who often give performances on the lawns in the area of the Cathedral. This man could not recognise any of his dancers and pointed out that it might be a north of England group as the 'Fool' was wearing a deer's head mask often worn by such groups. Set-back Number One. Next the Dean was shown the actual photograph and raised a very interesting problem; for although the building was clearly St. Albans Cathedral, the surroundings were completely different. The wrong trees, the lie of the land, the other buildings visible clearly indicated that the picture was a fake. Puzzled, our detective took a pause to review his position then showed the photograph to three more experts — a photographic expert, a country dance expert and a botanist. From these he gathered that the photograph was genuine, i.e. was not a fake and was printed on photograph paper of a type normally only available in the USA. The country dance man confirmed that the deer's head mask was a good clue to the group being a northern one but the colour of the shirts of the dancers together with the pattern of the strapping on the legs clearly indicated a Chilterns Group. He was not aware of any known group who wore such a strange mixture of styles and thought the whole group very fishy. The botanist looked at the photograph and made two important remarks. One, the grass was remarkably even and if he had to place bets, he would say it was plastic! And two of the trees in the background were of a type that would only survive the winter in the very South of England and were more likely to be found in southern USA than England. This made two references to the USA so our detective paid a visit to the American Travel Centre in London. Here, at last, he got his answer. The picture was taken at the 'Olde English Village' in a pleasure park in Miami. They even had a view of the scene, less dancers, to prove it. The grass was plastic and so was the Cathedral! After that the rest was easy.

This little, highly fictional, story illustrates the problems of the family historian in dealing with photographs. It is very difficult to get a correct answer unless one is an expert and the beginner can easily draw the wrong conclusion from a few vital facts.

The information which follows should be used with great caution because it is impossible to convey the years of experience necessary to interpret photographs in a few pages.

The definitive work on the British Service Uniform and Equipment during the First World War has yet to be written, hence anyone carrying out research has to glean evidence from a number of sources, none of which provide a quick or complete answer. Besides the few books given in the Bibliography, searches of Army Orders, Regimental Orders, Regimental Histories, Mobilisation Stores Tables (Army Form G 1029), the Photographic Collection of the IWM, and the many volumes of the various illustrated histories of the war can cast some light on the subject. There are also the experts such as the Staff of the NAM, the IWM and the few private enthusiasts who have spent many years studying the few sources available to build up a store of knowledge that is impossible to impart in a work of this nature. Most of the information given here is suitable for pictures of private soldiers and NCOs from the British Isles while serving in France. If you have doubts about these facts, it is best to ignore what follows as there were changes to uniform when going to other fronts and the various Empire Soldiers had similar, but not identical, uniforms.

Badges and Insignia

Photographs often show the ancestor in uniform wearing a multitude of badges which, if studied carefully, can, besides providing the obvious direct information on the meaning of the badge, give a rough date for the photograph.

The cap badge will identify the regiment or corps. Whole books have been written on this subject. Bibl. refs. 8 and 10 are inexpensive and can be found in most libraries. Bibl. ref. 13 is a very costly volume found only in the larger libraries but which is exhaustive in its coverage. With a few exceptions, the cap badge does not reveal the wearer's battalion, usually only the Regiment and even this may not be identifiable due to the unclearness of the picture. Usually, the badge is merely a white blob on the front of the cap and a careful comparison of the general outline of the blob with the many photographs in Bibl. ref 13 may be necessary in some cases. Some regiments wore a small badge on the lapels of the collar. These 'collar dogs' do not appear to have been common during the war, although most pre-war men would have had them. Maybe they were not issued to new recruits when supplies ran out. Bibl. ref.13 gives the best selection of collar badges but in general the form of the badge was based on the main feature or emblem of the cap badge, less its surrounding wreaths and garlands. The Royal Engineers and The Royal Artillery are two collar badges which are more frequently seen.

Should the picture show an outside view of the shoulder then another means of identification is available. Right at the top of the arm or, alternatively, on the button-down flap on the top of the shoulder, most regiments wore metal 'shoulder titles'. Many of these bore the number of the battalion (Bibl. ref. 15).

When in France, many Divisions adopted coloured patches of simple geometric design, i.e. square, triangle, circle, which were worn on the upper arm or on the shoulder epaulette as coloured fore and aft bands. These enabled men from different units from within the Division to be quickly identified at a distance. In some cases, they were confined to officers. Alternatively they were worn on the back of the tunic. There is no standard book on the subject, but Bibl. ref. 27 in the IWM gives many examples, although it is believed to be in error at times. Mr Chappell (Bibl. ref. 32) has an extensive card index on this subject. Bibl. ref. 23 gives details of Tank Corps badges.

The problem with the patches is that they were unofficial and the same patch and colour may have been used by different units in another Division. Even within a Division, the method of indicatmg Brigades/Battalions/Companies (even if any was used) varied from Division to Division, thus leading to much confusion both now and also during the war! Providing the regiment is positively known, then it may be possible to identify the exact battalion from the tab colours providing that they are visible, that the unit did in fact wear them, and the colours can be distinguished in a faded black and white photograph! However, the whole field is so complex that only an expert is likely to give the correct interpretation. Some units painted emblems on uipment and vehicles. These are to be found in Bibl. refs. 16, 18, 19, 24 and 27. The other badges on the arms of the uniform are more widespread in their use and for that matter far easier to distinguish. Between the elbows and the tops of both arms are the usual badges of rank. These consist of a number of 'Stripes' or 'Chevrons' with the point downwards: one for Lance Corporal, two for a Corporal, three for a Sergeant (Fig. 9). They remained unchanged throughout the war. The other badges are somewhat complex and changed several times during the war, hence a careful examination enables a photograph to be dated. Many of these used 'stripes' below the elbow. In nearly all cases, the points of the chevrons point towards the elbow joint. The ones above point down; the lower ones point upwards.

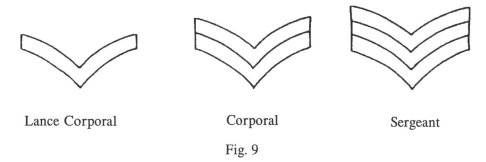

Lance Corporal   Corporal   Sergeant

Fig. 9

The badges of the Guards and of the Cavalry Regiments were more complex than those of the Infantry Regiments. (Check details in Bibl. ref. 4.)

The stripes on the forearm were of three types.

(a) Long Service/Good Conduct stripes (see Fig. 10). These were worn on the left arm, one stripe for two years, two stripes for six years, three stripes for 12 years, and four stripes for 18 years.

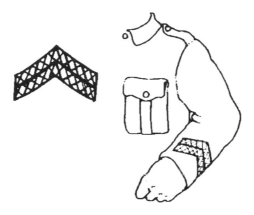

Fig. 10

These were in use throughout the war and anyone wearing two or more must have been a pre-war soldier in order to achieve the necessary six years service.

(b) Overseas service stripes. These were miniature inverted blue stripes near the cuff of the right sleeve. (Fig.11).

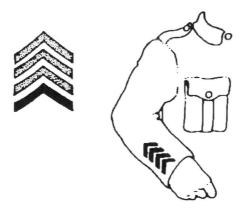

Fig. 11.

These were not introduced until 1st January 1918, hence any photograph showing them must have been taken after that date. The number of stripes indicated the number of years served overseas, but parts of a year, even one day, counted. Thus, if two stripes were worn, the man had at least one year and a day's service but less than two full years. If the first, the lowest, was earned before 31st December 1914, its colour was red. The colour difference can be detected in black and white photographs. Thus a man who arrived in France in November 1914, would, by February 1918, be entitled to five overseas service stripes, one red for 1914, three blue for 1915, 1916 and 1917, and one blue for the two months of 1918.

(c) Up to February 1915, various senior Sergeants wore four inverted stripes below the elbow. Thus all pictures showing this arrangement must have been taken before that date (Figs. 12–14).

Fig. 12. Four stripes: Quarter Master Sergeant or 1st Class Staff Sergeant.

Fig. 13. Four stripes plus a star: Regimental Quarter Master Sergeant.

Fig. 14. Four stripes plus a Crown: Quarter Master Corporal-Major and many similar ranks in the Household Cavalry. These were not normally worn on the jacket. Acting Sergeant Major on the permanent staff of the Territorial Force.

There were a number of variations to the rank chevrons. The Foot Guards superimposed a large rectangular badge partially covering the chevrons. This was surmounted by a Crown (Fig. 15, but see Bibl. ref. 4).

Fig.15.

Many Cavalry Regiments added a similar or circular badge either superimposed over the stripes, as with the Guards, or just above them, i.e. further up the arm (Fig. 16).

Fig. 16.

Other Corps added an important element of the corps badge just above the chevrons, i.e. higher up the arm as shown in Figs. 17–19.

Fig. 17. Company Sergeant Major, Royal Artillery.

Fig. 19. Company Sergeant Major, Royal Army Medical Corps. In this case, the Geneva Cross was worn by all RAMC ranks.

Fig. 18. Company Sergeant Major, Royal Engineers.

The appointment of Colour Sergeant (Figs. 20 and 21) was discontinued in February 1915. The flags are Union Jacks and should not be confused with the Signals Instructor (see Fig. 24).

Fig. 20. Colour Sergeant, Infantry Regiment.

Fig. 21. Colour Sergeant Rifle Regiment.

There was another type of badge on the arm which indicated a special skill above the normal standard. These were prize arm badges and would be awarded to expert shots, perhaps as a result of a competition within the regiment. A similar set of badges would be worn by men carrying out special jobs or trades, e.g. Saddlers. The prize arm badges tended to be dropped after the start of the war. There was little time to hold the competitions! A third set of similar badges was used to indicate instructors in particular skills (Figs. 22–24) (see Bibl. ref. 3).

Fig. 22. Instructor in Musketry.

Fig. 23. Gymnastic Instructor.

Fig. 24. Assistant Signalling Instructor.

These three types of badge were worn either on the forearm or on the upper arm above the rank chevrons. The precise meaning varied during the war and great care is required to determine whether a man was an instructor, tradesman or award wmner. A typical set of these badges is shown in Fig. 25.

Fig. 25. Appointment Badges. Usually worn on the upper right arm. The lyre with crown was worn by Bandmasters on the lower right arm. Left to right, top row: Bugler, Bugler (Rifle Corps), Trumpeter R.E. and R.A. up to about 1915/16, Trumpeter, Bandmaster. Bottom row: Bandsmen, Drummer (also Drum-Major, upper right), Gun Layer (also with 'O' – Observer), Trained Scout, a Trained Scout NCO had the bar.

Fig. 26. Instructors' Badges. Upper right arm (see also Figs. 22–24). Musketry; Gymnastic; Asst. Signaling; Gunnery (both upper arms) (with crown above and grenade below guns up to February 1915; with crown only or royal arms only after February 1915); Rough Rider, Riding Instructor or Remount Trainer.

Fig. 27. Prizes. Lower left arm. Upper row: Best Swordsman (lower right for Cavalry), Gunnery, Shooting (lower left or right). Lower row: Horse Driving, Gunnery (TF), Signalling. All except the last could appear with a star, a crown and/or a wreath.

Fig. 28. Skill-at-Arms. Usually lower left arm. Upper row: TF Proficiency Star (upper right, not much used after 1914), Lewis Gunner from 1917 (also 'HG' for Hotchkiss Gunner, 'MG' for Machine Gunner from 1914, 'R' for Range Taker), Volunteer Training Corps WWI 'Marksman'. Lower row: Infantry Bomber (upper right) from 1915 in red also in blue from January 1916 for Trench Mortar Gunner, TF Efficiency Diamond (on lower right), not often worn after 1914, four-pointed star TF NCOs proficiency badge also used by OTC but not much used after 1914. The five-pointed star was used by TF on lower right arm in groups of 1 to 6 stars.

Fig. 29. Trade Badges. Upper right arm. Wheelwright (also used for Carpenter), Pioneer, Saddler (for all horsed units), Smith (also artificer fitter, vehicle mechanic), Smith (farrier, both upper arms), Medical Orderly (not stretcher bearer who wore 'S.B.' arm band).

If the ancestor was a Warrant Officer, he would have worn one of many varieties of crowns, wreaths and coats of arms on the right lower arm.

The ranks were changed at least twice during the war, first in February 1915 and again in 1918.

The simple crown (Fig. 30) was used throughout the war although its meaning changed.

Fig. 30.

The crown and the wreath (Fig. 31) remained almost the same throughout the war but the rank the badge depicted changed in 1915 and 1918.

Fig. 31.

76

February 1915 saw the introduction of the coat of arms, and in 1918 a coat of arms in a wreath was introduced (Figs. 32 and 33).

Fig. 32.

Fig. 33.

The Bandmaster's Lyre remained throughout the war (see Fig. 25).

The exact meaning of the rank indicated by the badges can only be determined by reference to Army Orders and Bibl. refs. 4 and 14.

The Guards Regiments and the Household Cavalry are noted for variations in the badges of rank. Check with Bibl. ref. 4.

Arm Bands

Various Staff Officers wore arm bands to indicate the branch of the army with which they served but numerous bands were worn by other ranks and, since they were easily removed from the uniform, frequently turn up 1n family archives.

Description	Where Worn	Meaning
Red armband with 'PM'	Right arm	Provost Marshal
Red armband with 'APM'	Right arm	Assistant Provost Marshal
Blue and White bands	Both arms	Signal Service
Red band		Runner
Black 'MP' on Red band (sometimes White or yellow)	Right arm	Military Police
'GMP'		Garrison Military Police
Black 'RTO' on white band	Right arm	Rail Transport Officer
Black 'Embark' on white band	Right arm	Embarkation Staff
Yellow	Both arms	Servant to Military Attaché
Red 'SB' on White	Right arm	Stretcher Bearer
Green	Both arms	Press
Khaki with Red Crown		A *Derby* man awaiting call up (worn in civvies)
Blue	Right arm	Convalescent soldier
'NR'		National Reserve
'GR' on red	Left arm	Volunteer Training Corps before December 1916
Black and White vertical stripes with *Press*		Press Officer

RAMC Nursing Orderlies wore horizontal red bars on the cuff, one for Second Class Orderly, two for First Class Orderly.

Identity Tags

By the end of the war, each man wore two, one red, one green. If the soldier was killed the red one was taken with his pay book for the records. The green tag was left on the body for identity purposes.

Wound Stripes and Silver Badge

In August 1916, a vertical 2-inch-long stripe was approved for those who had been wounded since 4th August 1914. These were worn on the cuff of the left arm. More than one could be worn.

After July 1917, their use was extended to Military Nurses and VADs. Men discharged during the war were issued with a circular lapel badge with the inscription *For King and Empire — Services Rendered* (see Fig. 34). It was first issued in September 1916. All those entitled to a Badge have the fact included on their Medal Roll Index Card which is available on microfiche at the PRO, Kew. There is a separate set of fiche for women recipients.

Fig. 34.

Uniform and Equipment

With care, some information can be obtained from the man's uniform and equipment. Equipment is loosely defined as the various belts, straps, and haversacks carried by the soldier as opposed to the clothing.

Items of variance can be listed as follows:
caps (many types)
gas masks (many types)
belts (many types)
ammunition pouches
trousers, kilt
puttees (methods of wearing)
boots

In general, the photographs in the hands of the family show the ancestor in his 'walking out dress' or, to be more precise, his *only* uniform (less most of the equipment) cleaned and pressed to look its best. Many photographers made a living taking pictures of the soldiers in their first uniform, at camps and depots as groups were passed out. On the continent, French photographers set up backcloths in the street to tempt the young lads to have a picture taken to send home to the family. Private cameras were banned shortly after the start of the war but many pictures were taken in spite of this and these, although often unclear, show a more informal aspect of the soldier's life. It is here that the background can give a few more clues.

The khaki uniform was introduced in 1908 as a 'working' or 'fighting' outfit to wear instead of the elaborate walking out and formal uniforms. It was thus treated by the old Regulars of 1914 as a pair of overalls which were not worth the care given to the proper uniform. With the outbreak of the war, the formal uniforms went into store and the Service Drab became the only one seen for several years. The new recruits to the Service Battalion copied the sloppy habits of the Regulars as regards the service dress and the general smartness of the troops was not helped by the motley collection of woolly hats and British 'warms' introduced during 1915. As the war progressed, however, pride in the uniform increased so that by 1918–19 many men had had their uniforms 'modified' to improve the fit and to introduce small items of individuality. The German tailors made a good income from the British Rhine Army during 1919.

Starting at the feet, the following points may help to identify a soldier's job if not his corps or regiment.

Boots and Puttees

The 'standard' kit for the lower part of the legs was the leather ankle boot with a strip of khaki cloth wound around the shins between the knee and the ankle; the puttee. This was the standard uniform of all those who moved on foot be they infantry or part of the vast force helping behind the front. The winding of the puttees was important. The infantry man wound his from the ankle up, finishing with the narrower fastening tapes tied at the top. Those associated with horses, like the Artillery, who used horses to pull the guns and, of course, the Cavalry, started at the top and fastened at the ankle. The tapes in this case were partly hidden by the leather front to the spurs which they frequently wore even when 'walking out', especially to the nearest photographer's. The Cavalry style puttees were one of the marks of individuality adopted by some infantry men. In the latter stages of the war, various patterns were produced by twisting the strip as it was wound. These can be seen in pictures as diagonal lines or diamond shapes on the sides of the legs. Although frowned upon when on duty, it was just the thing to impress the family or girlfriend when on leave.

Cavalry men did not, as a rule, wear riding boots, which were worn by the officer and perhaps the senior NCOs. Those who drove horse transport usually rode on the leading horse rather than sitting on the cart or gun carriage. For this purpose, they wore a very heavy leather gaiter on the right leg. This had a narrow, vertical rubbing strip on the outside and three straps fastened in front by buckles. This device protected the driver's leg from being crushed between the horses.

Motorcyclists had a lighter leather gaiter or big riding boots.

Highland Regiments and various expatriate battalions, such as the London Scottish, wore the kilt. With this, socks were worn. In the early days of the war, the tops of the boots and the lower part of the legs were covered in light-coloured canvas spats. These were very unsuitable for front line wear and were soon replaced by puttees; at a later date, a special short puttee was introduced. For the London Scottish, Bibl. ref. 6 gives detailed information. This states that, at the start of the war, even shoes were worn as they 'looked neater with spats'. Normal puttees were introduced in 'autumn 1914' and the short ones' in 1916. The kilted Scottish Regiments also wore stocking tops with a variety of plain or coloured patterns with garter tabs projecting below the turned over tops on the outside of the legs. Again, Bibl. ref. 6 refers to the fact that the London Scottish wore their tabs pushed round towards the front so that the forward edge was in line with the shin bone from July 1917 onwards.

At this point it might be interesting to note that the British soldier of 1914—18 travelled light, at least as far as clothes were concerned. He had only one uniform and for that matter only one of everything except two pairs of underpants (drawers, woollen), two shirts and three pairs of socks. Highland Regiments had a kilt instead of trousers and they were issued with no underpants. Various overalls, warm leather jackets, etc. were available for special jobs as well as many unofficial items of comfort.

Trousers

The trousers were of two main types.

(a) Khaki serge trousers without turnups for those who fought on foot.

(b) A pair of cord pantaloons used by mounted units which were rather fuller than the normal serge trousers issued to those who fought on foot. The former sometimes had leather pads on the inside of the leg. These differences are often difficult to spot in a faded photograph. Trousers were sometimes cut off at the knee to produce a pair of shorts. These were worn in France more as a protection from lice than for the heat.

Kilts

The Highland Regiments wore kilts which were covered, in many cases, by a leather apron. The sporran was a poor version of the full dress version worn before the war but can be used to identify some of the regiments. In general, pipers and other musicians wore a more elaborate dress. This frequently included 'diced' stocking tops. Sergeants wore the 'sgian dubh/skean-dhu' (dagger) in the stockings. The various plaids enable the expert to identify and date photographs of Scottish troops.

Lowland Regiments wore trews and in France this meant normal Service Dress, the more formal uniform having been left at home for the duration of the war.

Highland Light Infantry Royal Scots King's Own Scottish Borderers Royal Scots Fusiliers The Cameronians (Scottish Rifles)	wore trews, i.e. trousers of a tartan material

The Black Watch (Royal Highlanders)
    Five short black tassels in two rows
    on a white horsehair sporran
Seaforth Highlanders
    Two long black tassels on a
    white horsehair sporran
Gordon Highlanders
    Two long black tassels on a
    white horsehair sporran
The Queen's Own Cameron Highlanders
    Two long white tassels on a
    black sporran
Princess Louise's (Argyll and Sutherland
    Highlanders)
    Six short tassels on the sporran

wore the kilt. A description of the sporran is given although it was not always worn in France.

Belts

Many different types of belt were issued in the years prior to the war. Before 1903, belts had a buckle with a large round appearance some of which had a regimental motif although this cannot usually be discerned in a photograph (Fig. 43). Ammunition was carried in two large leather pouches of the Slade Wallace pattern. These were similar to Fig. 41 but much lighter in appearance although the white leather was sometimes stained with tea to darken it. In 1914, some units of auxiliary troops (e.g. the RAMC) were still wearing these round buckle belts but it is believed that this was confined to a few pre-war regulars. The large white pouches were rarely seen but may have been given to a few of the 'Kitchener' Volunteers for training purposes. Besides the normal pattern with the flap and buckle outside, there was another later type with the fastening on the inside nearest the soldier's belt which opened upwards and outwards.

In 1903, a new design was introduced which had a brown leather belt with a rectangular brass buckle with one prong (Fig. 36). The buckle used by officers was similar but had two prongs (Fig. 37). Ammunition was carried in two ways; in small pouches which fitted to the belt and in pouches held on a diagonal belt running from the left shoulder to the waist on the right side. This belt and equipment continued in use right through the war for some types of unit. Men who did not normally need to carry a rifle, such as lorry and wagon drivers and RAMC men, wore this waist belt

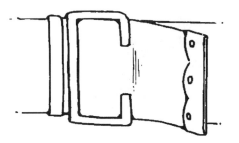

Fig. 35. '1908 Webbing' Buckle.

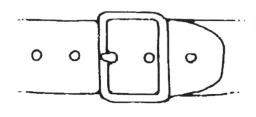

Fig. 36. '1903 Leather' Buckle.

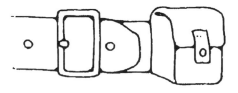

Fig. 37. Officers' Buckle.

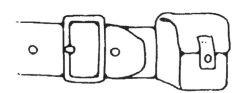

Fig. 38. '1903 Leather' ammunition pouch. Only one shown.

Fig. 39. '1903 Leather' with pistol ammunition pouch.

Fig. 40. '1914 Leather' Buckle.

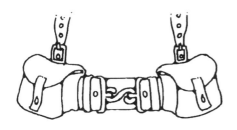

Fig. 41. '1914 Leather' with ammunition pouches.

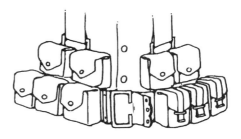

Fig. 42. '1908 Webbing' ammunition pouches with post-October 1914 straps.

Fig. 43. The 1888 belt still used up to 1914. The leather was white.

Fig. 44. The box respirator of 1916 onwards. The Cavalry had a modified version with the left-hand strap attached along the side seam just above the left-hand 'D' ring.

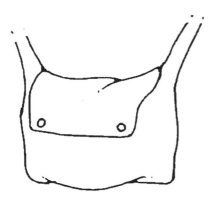

Fig. 45. One of the early gas masks.

Fig. 46. The standard 1908 haversack which was in use throughout the war period.

83

without any pouches (Fig. 38). Although not worn when working, most of these men were tradesmen rather than fighting men and they used the belt to smarten up the uniform when posing for photographs. A similar belt was worn with a small semicircular pouch and a pistol holder (Fig. 39)g. This would be worn by many NCOs, particularly those involved with horses in transport units. The diagonal bandolier was used by cavalry when it carried five pouches in the front and 4 four more down the back. Others involved with both the fighting and horses wore the bandolier but only with the five front pouches. The bandolier was nearly always worn, without the waist belt, when posed photographs were taken. In general, these units continued to wear the 1903 belts until the end of the war although most cavalry men were re-equipped when transferred to Infantry Regiments. Other users of the 1903 waist belt were later issued with webbing belts. These included military police and machine gunners, both of whom wore pistols, and despatch motorcyclists. A version of the 1903 bandolier with very wide pouches was used by Cavalry Hotchkiss machine gunners.

In 1908, the webbing belt and equipment had been tntroduced. This was the normal equipment used through the war by most soldiers. The wide webbing waist belt with its distinctive buckle with a gap in its vertical frame side is easy to spot (Fig. 35). The ammunition was carried in five webbing pouches in two rows on each side (Fig. 42). These pouches were closed by simple flaps held down by press studs. In October 1914 this was changed. The flaps on the lower three pouches on the left side were held down by a narrow webbing strap fastened to the pouch at the bottom which, after passing up the front, was held by a press stud on the top of the pouch.

Any picture showing the original version was almost certainly taken very early in the war. Unfortunately, most posed photographs were taken without the pouches but with the belt.

When the war broke out, the manufacturers could not produce enough sets of webbing equipment so, as a temporary measure, in 1914 leather was introduced. This had a dark brown leather belt with an 'S'-shaped clasp (Fig. 40). Ammunition was carried in two large dark brown leather pouches, one on each side (Fig. 41), which were similar in appearance to the 1888 Slade Wallace equipment. In photographs this dark brown leather appears to be almost black. This leather equipment was issued to many units training in England but it was used by many TF troops in Gallipoli and it reached France by 1916 although not in large numbers. The Tank Corps used a version in 1917.

The Mobilisation Stores Tables G 1029 (Bibl. ref. 31), found in some Museums and in the Army Forms Collection in the IWM 'Box G', give a description of the equipment issued to each unit. They include a list of the number and type of Belt (1903 or 1908) as well as the number of pouches. A comparison with the list of personnel will enable the researcher to see that NCOs and/or WOs frequently had a pistol instead of a rifle. Although the tables were frequently updated, they showed what the unit should have, not what they did in fact wear. If the storekeeper had no stock of the specified equipment then the whole unit would be issued with what was available.

Jackets

Only two types were in general use during the war, the normal khaki jacket and the modified one used by Scottish Regiments. The normal jacket had five buttons down the front with the belt, if worn, sitting between the lower two. The buttons were normally brass but the Rifle Regiments had black buttons. Below the belt level there were two large pockets closed at the top by a buttoned-down flap. Above the waist were two smaller pockets, one on each breast closed by similar flaps and buttons. These had box pleats down the centre. Above the pockets were the 'rifle patches', pieces of cloth sewn on to the jacket to cover the area between the top of the pocket and the shoulder where the butt of the rifle would press when fired.

In 1914, with the shortage of uniforms, an economy version was made in which the top pockets had no box pleats and the rifle patches were missing. Frequently the buttons were plain, i.e. they had no regimental insignia or Royal Coat of Arms. This uniform was common in 1915 and 1916 but was seldom seen in 1917 or later. In the early days of the war, a dark blue uniform was also worn. This had a fold-flat 'fore and aft' forage cap similar to that used in WWII. This uniform was used only in the UK although some were worn by British POWs in Germany. Wounded soldiers wore a very loose light blue uniform similar to a pair of pyjamas. The white shirt and red tie as well as a blue arm band are plainly visible in photographs. The Scottish Regiments wore a jacket which was cut away at the front below the waist so as to clear the sporran.

Gas Masks

A soldier's equipment included a water bottle worn on the right side and a haversack worn on the left side. On the back was the Pack and a 'D'-shaped canteen in a canvas container. The 1903 equipment had no pack but the greatcoat and kit were rolled up and carried on the back, high on the shoulders. Cavalry men and others with the diagonal bandolier carried the greatcoat in a long roll over one shoulder. Most of this equipment did not appear in family photographs. However, the introduction of gas in the spring of 1915 brought another item for the soldier to carry even when off duty in areas far behind the lines — the gas mask. This included visits to the photographers. Hence the gas mask container can be used for dating. Many different types were introduced in rapid succession until the arrival of the 'box respirator' in June 1916.

The early gas masks were carried in shapeless bags over the shoulder (Fig. 45). The box respirator of 1916 had a rectangular canvas bag about 9" × 9" × 2" with sharp edges and corners (Fig. 44). The top was closed by a short flap held down by two press studs. (The haversack was of similar size but somewhat thicker. The top flap reached half-way down the side and was held down by two straps (Fig. 46).) The box respirator remained substantially unchanged for the rest of the war. In fact, the

1939—45 service gas mask is very similar. It could be worn slung from the shoulder, tied to the chest with the aid of two small D-shaped rings sewn to the sides, or on top of the pack behind the head. True Cavalry men wore a modified box respirator with the straps on one side mounted half-way down the side of the satchel (Bibl. ref. 33).

Hats and Caps

In 1914 all soldiers (except Highlanders) had a flat-topped peaked khaki cap. This can be recognised by its sharp edges; the flat top had a circular metal spring or ring inserted inside to hold the circular top rigid and taut. The leather strap could be unfastened and placed under the chin to retain the cap when on horse back. Once in France, the metal spring was frequently removed so that the top edge became less defined. During the winter, numerous unofficial hats, caps and balaclavas were introduced. By the winter of 1915/16 a new soft cap was introduced and the rigid one was on its way out. This new soft cap still had its flat circular top and peak but the edges were so poorly defined that it appeared like a tam-o'-shanter with a peak. To each side, a long ear flap was fitted. These were normally worn pulled up and buttoned together on the top of the cap, forming a two and a half inch wide band running from side to side across the top.

In October 1915, tin hats began to appear but were only issued to those in the trenches and were transferred to the fresh men at the end of a turn of duty. By June 1916, almost every man had his own and it had to be carried on one's person if within 10—15 miles of the front line. Hence it is often seen in photographs. In 1917, a type of tin helmet with a chain mesh face veil was issued to some troops. During the winter of 1915/16, yet another soft cap was introduced. This was a reversion to the style of the 1914 rigid flat cap but without stiffeners. The cap badge pushed up the front edge of the flat top into a shallow point. The peak itself was stiffened slightly by rows of stitching which can be seen in clear photographs. As this cap could be put into the pack when wearing the tin helmet, it soon lost any smartness it had. The dark blue forage-type fold-flat cap used in the early days of the war has already been mentioned.

Highland Troops.

Scottish troops saw many changes of head gear. At the outbreak of war, only the Scots Guards had the flat-top service cap and this was dark blue with a red, white and green diced band around it. It had no chin straps. The other Regiments, both Highland and Lowland, wore a blue glengarry. This was rather similar to the 'fore and aft' cap worn during WWII but somewhat broader. Some regiments had diced bands. Others wore a small pom-pom (the tourie) in the middle of the crown.

Black Watch. Blue glengarry, no band, red tourie.

Argyll and Sutherland Highlanders. Blue glengarry, red and white diced band.

Cameronians. Dark green glengarry, no band, black tourie.

Other Regiments. Blue engarry, red, white and dark green band.

The glengarry was soon abandoned and a very full tam-o'-shanter issued. This was so full that it fell all over the place and, after attempts to stiffen it with a circular spring which gave it an almost comic appearance, this too was replaced. Its successor was the Balmoral bonnet. This was also a tam-o'-shanter but not nearly so full. It had been adopted by most regiments by spring 1915.

The whole question of Scottish uniform is a matter for an expert.

Other Units

The Royal Naval Division started the war with blue naval caps then changed to khaki naval caps; at a later date, normal soldiers' caps were issued.

Despatch Riders

Some motor cycle despatch riders had a very high crowned, peaked cap which had pleats round the side. It gives the appearance of a mob cap with a peak.

Greatcoats

These came in two types, a short double-breasted version for mounted men and a single-breasted one of longer length for the others. There were other coats but these were not of general issue. Several types of sheepskin jacket were available both with the fur inside and outside. Some despatch riders (motor cycle) wore a short mackintosh with a large storm collar, with or without leggings and gloves.

General

Although the style of uniform and type of equipment was laid down, shortages of equipment meant that many units, particularly at the start of the war, used non-standard equipment, 1914 leather instead of 1908 webbing. Attempts were made to ensure each unit went overseas with 1908 webbing but many TF units had been equipped with 1914 leather and fought in Gallipoli still wearing it. In general, front-line troops had the correct equipment and if any man of a group had to have alternative equipment then all the men had it. However, the British soldier is noted for his skill in making unpopular kit wear out very quickly while favourite items were always in good condition, particularly if orders stated they were to be changed when worn out!

Bibliography

(1) *1913 Edition of the 1908 Webbing Regulations,* IWM.
(2) *1914 Edition of the 1914 Clothing Regulations,* IWM.
(3) *British Army Proficiency Badges,* by Denis Edwards and David Langley, The Sherwood Press, 1984.
(4) Badges of Warrant and Non-Commissioned Officers, by N.P. Dawney, in *The Special Publication of Society for Army Historica§Research,* No. 6, 1949, NAM.
(5) *Scottish Military Uniforms,* by R. Wilkinson-Latham, David and Charles, 1970.
(6) *Uniform of the London Scottish 1859–1959,* by J.O. Robson, London Scottish Regiment, Ogilby Trust, 1960.

(7) *The ABC of the Army,* by Captain J. Atkinson, Gale and Polden, 1914. Gives details of 1914 style badges, etc.

(8) *Badges of the British Army 1820–1960,* by F. Wilkinson, Arms and Armour Press.

(9) *Buttons of the British Army 1855–1960,* by Howard Ripley, Arms and Armour Press.

(10) *Cavalry and Yeomanry Badges of the British Army 1914,* by F. Wilkinson, Arms and Armour Press.

(11) *Scottish Regimental Badges 1793–1971,* by W.H. Bloomer, Arms and Armour Press.

(12) Trade Badges of the British Army, in *Journal of the Military Historical Society,* Vol. XXX, No. 119, Feb 1980.

(13) *Military Badges of the British Empire 1914–18,* by R.H.W. Cox, Benn, 3,000 photographs, 325 pp.

(14) *Badges and Insignia of the British Armed Forces,* by Major W.Y. Carmen, Adam and Chas. Black, 1944.

(15) *Collecting Medal Shoulder Titles,* by R.A. Westlake, Warne, 1980.

(16) *Army, Corps and Divisional Signs 1914–18.* Three Sets of cigarette cards by Players circa 1925, two sets of 50 and one set of 100.

(17) *Badges and their Meaning,* Geo. Philips and Son Ltd.,1917(?).

(18) *A List of some ASC Emblems and Flashes,* WO161/13, PRO, Kew.

(19) *Photos of Emblems, etc., Q31366-83,* IWM Photograph Library.

(20) *Men at Arms No. 81, The British Army 1914–18,* by D.S.V.Fosten and R.J. Marrion, Osprey Series.

(21) *Army Uniforms of World War I,* by A. Mollo, Blandford Press.

(22) *Army Orders 1912–19,* IWM.

(23) *Tank and AFV Crew Uniforms since 1916,* by Martin Windrow.

(24) The Formation Sign, in *Journal of the Military Heraldry Society,* IWM Library.

(25) The Uniform of the Volunteers, 1914–19, by E.J. Martin, in *Journal of the Society for Army Historical Research,* Vol. XVI, No. 67, Autumn 1983.

(26) *Family History in Focus,* edited by D. Steel and L. Taylor, Lutterworth Press, 1984.

(27) *British Formation Signs,* by John Waring, Section 2, IWM. Ref.06 (41) 7:02/1).

(28) *Men at Arms, No. 107, British Infantry Equipment 1808-1908,* by Mike Chappell, Osprey Series.

(29) *Men at Arms, No. 108, British Infantry Equipment 1908-1980,* by Mike Chappell, Osprey Series.

(30) A collection of paintings by A.E. Haswell Miller, IWM Art Collection Ref. Nos.4102-4206, shows many men in typical uniforms. These paintings are the results of a survey made in 1919–20 on the modifications to uniforms, Ref. 182.521. This is in very poor condition and will not be available for inspection for several years (as at 1986).

(31) Mobilisation Stores Tables (IWM Forms Collection G1098) gives details of the type of equipment laid down for each type of unit. There is no guarantee that the stores actually had the equipment of that type when it was issued.

(32) *Family History News and Digest,* Vol.6, No. 2. September 1987. Gives details of experts able to identify photographs.

(33) *Men at Arms, No. 138, British Cavalry Equipment 1800–1941,* by Mike Chappell, Osprey Series.

13

ARMY ADMINISTRATION

As with any large organisation, the Army required a number of rules and regulations in order that it could be efficiently administered. These rules provide the family historian with information on badges, dates for the formation of units, conditions of service and pay.

King's Reglations

The army's 'Standing Orders'. They provide the rules that govern a soldier's life in the army. The issue at the outbreak of war was the 1912 edition, a copy of which is available in the IWM Library. King's Regulations were revised by the monthly issue of Army Orders, which usually contained a list of alterations.

Army Orders

Besides the routine updating of King's Regulations, the monthly booklets provided orders dealing with the introduction of new badges, medals and changes in rank. Pre-war issues listed the proposed rotas of the Regular Battalions. Wartime issues included details of the formation of the new VAD and Volunteer Training Corps Units. Other regular features were the lists of new army books, training manuals, etc. Changes in Mobilisation Stores Tables and the introduction of new ones for recently formed types of units were noted.

Of more direct interest to the family historian are the lists of Long Service Medal Awards and Citations for the more important Gallantry Medals. The issues of Army Orders are bound up in yearly volumes, each with an mdex although this should be used with care as an order might be amended by a later one. It takes a long time to determine the true history of any one item. A full set of Army Orders is in the IWM Library and in the PRO, Kew (WO123/. . .).

Regimental Orders

Regiments, Corps and Battalions also issued orders which dealt with routine matters and included the names of those promoted. Those of the larger units, i.e. Corps, were frequently printed and could cover many aspects of running an organisation of some two or three hundred thousand men. The intricate arrangement of ASC pay scales can be found in the printed orders (ASC orders 1916 CO52 and CO53). Orders were classed as Part I and Part II, Part II being an extract of Part I containing those items that would be passed to army HQ to inform the Records Officer of changes in rank and pay and similar details. When visiting a Regimental Museum, the Orders are one of the documents that should be sought.

Army Council Instructions

Another monthly series which appears to be very similar to Army Orders. Starting at the outbreak of the war, they were at first numbered in sequence starting anew each month. By 1916, they had changed the system and this sequence ran through a full year from January to December by which time the number exceeded 2,000. The early issues were indexed by each month but by 1916 each six monthly bound volume had its index, the one at the end of the July–December volume covering the full year, i.e. two volumes. The range of subjects covered was immense:

ACI 41/Aug/1914, issued three days after the outbreak of war, was the highly appropriate instruction calling upon each battalion to send a number of officers and NCOs to the depot in order to train the thousands of volunteers that were queuing outside the recruiting offices. The succeeding instruction, *ACI 43/Aug/1914*, whilst of great importance, appears at first glance to be very trivial. It gave instructions that men be trained to mend their socks!

Among the data to be found buried within the nine or ten volumes and some ten or twelve thousand instructions that covered the war period are lists of dates for founding the 'Pals' Battalions and the other locally formed units. With the arrival of conscription, a monthly list informed Recruiting Officers of the number of men to be sent to which Regiment and Training Depot, a list which changed each month from February 1916 onwards. In December 1916 and at the start of 1917, a series of ACIs lists the regimental numbers to be allocated to the various TF Units. In some cases it may enable the researcher to pinpoint the ancestor's unit at once. Other useful information can be gleaned from the instructions on training syllabuse and medical grades of recruits. A set of ACIs running from August 1914 has recently become available in the PRO, Kew WO293/1 et seq.

When dealing with Parish Records, the researcher has his questions answered by books such as Tate's *Parish Chest*. With the Army, failing the existence of an equivalent text book, these Regulations and Orders can provide the sources that must be searched. The existence of a set of Regimental Orders for the ancestor's unit may even provide his name.

14

LOCAL LIBRARIES AND COUNTY RECORD OFFICES

Most large towns have a library which contains a Local History or Archive Department. These could well have copies of the 'standard' Regimental Histories for the local Regiments. Any lists of soldiers such as school Rolls of Service and Rolls of Honour, similar records for local firms and printed Town Rolls are also likely to be held.

Local Volunteer Training Corps Units should also feature in the collection, perhaps with photographs. Their weekly orders, with names, appear in the local newspaper. The same files will hold details of the various camps in the area; back copies of local newspapers are usually held, if only on microfilm.

The CROs in general duplicate the library collections even in the area of printed Regimental Histories. They do, however, sometimes hold a number of classes of documents referring to soldiers or the Great War in general. Some offices hold the records of the County TF Associations. Most of the records are involved with the administration of the Force but a few can include names of men. A few CROs hold records from Regular Battalions as well. Nearly all hold records of the post-1834 Poor Law Unions and for Urban Councils. These authorities were responsible for the Tribunals held to hear appeals against the 1916 conscription. The appeals against the decisions of these Tribunals are usually held on a county basis but may be closed for 100 years. However, they may have been reported in the local newspaper. The same applies to the Local Tribunals. The PRO, Kew, has a number of documents on these Conscientious Objectors, including records of many Middlesex men (see indexes in MH47/136–141). Other records on Conscientious Objectors, as well as many books on the subject, are held at the Library of the Society of Friends (The Quakers), Euston Road, London. The civil parish records may contain papers of the War Memorial Committee, the various Welfare Committees and lists of Servicemen prepared for various purposes.

Some ROs have prepared lists or indexes covering the Great War, but use them with care. Check by examination if it contains references to documents held in Civil Parish Collections or only those held in special war collections. Town Clerks' papers or records are another source worth searching.

It is always worth checking the Regimental History or E.A. James *British Regiments 1914-18* for information on where the various battalions were raised, trained or stationed within the UK. Many regiments had training areas miles away from the 'county of origin'. Whilst the Local History Library or CRO may have some 'official' records of the regiment, it is possible that other information may be held in the library local to the training area.

Those having ancestors in the 12th or 13th (Transport Workers) Battalion of the Beds and Herts might well glean a few facts from the Croydon area where the battlions were formed in December 1916 and where they remained throughout the war.

The HQ of the ASC was at Woolwich but they had a large depot for training motor transport personnel at Grove Park in SE London. A search of the local libraries would locate *A History of Grove Park in the Great War* by John King. This deals in great detail with the ASC depot and quotes extracts from the local newspaper, *The Lee Journal* (yet another clue to follow up), which mentions the names of ASC drivers involved in a number of traffic accidents. The book also includes a number of photographs which are not to be found in either the ASC Museum or the IWM.

In 1922, The Local War Records Committee was set up by the London School of Economics and Political Science for an *Economic History Survey of the War Period.* A questionnaire was sent to all councils, etc. A check of the documents listed in it reveals that many are still in CROs, although in 1922 many records had not been deposited.

15

LISTS OF MEN

Any family historian aims to find his ancestor in a list, be it a parish register or a census. With 1914 army ancestors, the lists are few and, in most cases, too short.

The lists can be considered in two groups. Firstly, those dealing with the man as a soldier, which often associate him with his unit, be it regiment or corps. Secondly, those drawn up by civil bodies and these usually group him with his peacetime associates although his military details may still be gtven.

Military Lists
List of War Dead

Soldiers died in the Great War 1914–18, HMSO, 1920, 80 volumes; does not give precise place of death. A copy on microfilm at PRO, Kew, near WO100/...films.

List of War Dead in the Care of the Commonwealth War Graves Commission

This frequently details next of kin, and the location of the grave, if any, gives a clue as to where he was killed. This in turn may help to identify a precise corps unit which was in that area at that date. Beware of 'died of wounds' entries as he may have died many miles from the front. A small charge is now made for searching the records.

Lists of Dead in the care of the regiment or corps (Roll of Honour)

These may give a precise location at the time of death.

Lists of Wounded

In the case of a regiment or corps, only a few exist but when they do, they provide the vital proof that may not exist elsewhere.

'Official' Casualty List in Local and National Newspapers

In the early days of the war these lists gave details of the Regiment but by 1916 even this information was deleted in order to prevent the Germans obtaining too much assistance. Although issued regularly by the Assistant Adjutant General's Office, they were not always published by the papers, at least not in their entirety. 'Local' names were extracted and published by the local newspapers. Officers' names appeared after about three weeks, men's names took somewhat longer, six weeks. Post-1917 lists are available at several large libraries.

Army Service Records

Most of these were destroyed during the last War. Those that survived are held by the Ministry of Defence at Hayes and can be searched upon payment of a fee. The records are now being filmed and the films will be made available at the Public Record Office, Kew as each initial letter is completed. See Section 1 for details.

Medal Rolls

A microfiche index is held at PRO, Kew, for all those entitled to a medal. The records in WO329/. . . give very little information but sometimes give the date of wounding, death, going overseas or of discharge.

See PRO Leaflet No. 101 *Service Medal and Award Rolls: War of 1914—18* and PRO Leaflet No. 105 *First World War: Indexes to Medal Entitlement.*

Family Records Centre, Myddelton Place

The Registers in the Miscellaneous Section give all those who died. Names are listed in one alphabetical sequence. The usual certificates are available at normal cost.

War Diaries

Almost every unit kept a War Diary but these very seldom mentioned men's names. Women nurses were nearly always recorded as they arrived or left the unit. Many Base Hospitals listed men who died, particularly officers. (Deaths in Base Hospitals were infrequent.)

Medical Records

A small sample of records remains in the PRO, Kew MN106/. . . (see Section 10 for details).

Regiment, Battalion or Unit Nominal Rolls

From printed books (see below) and Regimental Museums or CROs. Very few are now extant. A few units have embarkation rolls of all those who sailed for France, others have lists of men compiled for special purposes, such as the issue of items of clothing, leave or rifle practice, company employ books, Minor Offence Reports, Rail Warrant Counterfoils. A number of Nominal Rolls may still be held by the Ministry of Defence as finding aids to other documents but these are unlikely to be released before the main series of soldiers' documents.

Printed Books

Regimental Histories frequently list awards and/or those killed, seldom all those who served. Battalion or unit histories, on the other hand, often have complete lists as the number of men per unit was much smaller but the books are rare. One book on a Yeomanry Regiment has no complete roll but includes the 'runners and riders' at the regimental horse race.

Records still in Regimental Care

These are confined to the Guards Regiment and the Household Cavalry. A very few regiments have 'unofficial' lists or card indexes compiled from many sources which may or may not be complete. Similar lists are held by a few private individuals. The Officer Training Units, The Honourable Artillery Company and the Artists Rifles have records of the trainees who passed through the unit.

Town Lists

Some towns formed Local or 'Pals' Battalions. The men who volunteered for service in these battalions are sometimes listed in printed books published by the town.

Recruiting Books

These exist for a large area of Surrey but are probably not complete (Surrey CRO Kingston-upon-Thames). Also, a very few are still with the regiments (see Section 11).

Private Diaries

Many soldiers kept diaries and these freuently name the writer's friends (Regimental Museum, IWM, CROs, Local Library).

Private Autograph Books

A valuable source of names but as the books are still in private hands they are difficult to find.

Field Pocket Books

Officers carried a small note book. Some of them have survived and list names of men killed or wounded as well as men under the officer's command (CROs, Regimental Museum, private hands).

County Territorial Force Association

This is the organisation which controlled the Territorial Battalion of the County Regiment, also the Yeomanry Regiment and the Volunteer Training Corps. Minute Books and Accounts are often in the CRO and these sometimes include lists of men.

Civil Lists

Church Magazines

These frequently published lists of parishioners in the forces (CRO, local library, the Church).

Church Orders of Service

Service sheets on 'days of prayer' frequently listed men.

Village, Town and Church War Memorial Unveiling

Order of Service. Service Sheets frequently listed those names on the Memorial plus all who served although they might not be named on the Memorial.

Records of Local Military Service Tribunal

The tribunals dealt with those who applied for exemption from the 1916 Conscription Act. The records often contain family detail but no military information as the man was not yet in the army. Papers may be in CRO or see report in the local newspaper. Tribunals were held within Poor Law Union areas, Urban District and Borough Councils. Records of Middlesex men are in the PRO, MH47/136–141. Other records are held at the Library of The Society of Friends (The Quakers), Euston Road, London.

Records of Appeals Tribunal

Contain appeals to Military Service Tribunal held on a county basis. Proceedmgs may be closed for 100 years, but check for report in local press.

War Memorial Committees

The Committees were formed to erect a memorial to the dead and/or all who served from a village, parish or town. Papers often list names of the men (CRO).

War Distress Welfare Committees

They were organised by towns, villages and parishes to help war widows and wives, children of soldiers, etc. Correspondence and minute books in CRO.

War Pension Committee; Soldiers, Sailors Families Association; Soldiers, Sailors Help Society

Records at CRO.

Welcome Home Committee

The papers often include lists of men. Records at CRO.

1915 National Registration

This was a census to find possible recruits as well as war munitions workers. It is believed to have been destroyed. Check CROs but none have reported having lists. Some CROs have associated papers.

POW Fund Committees

Voters Lists

The Electoral Roll for an army camp will include members of the permanent staff. Trainees and other transient personnel had no residence qualification for pre-1918 Rolls. This was abolished in 1918 and hence a large number of men were included. No army rank or number was given (CRO, local library).

Absentee Voters List

For 1918 and 1919 only, gives full details of rank, number and unit (CRO, local library). (See Section 8.)

Rolls of Honour

Many firms issued lists of serving men, as did towns and villages. The local library and CRO may have some but many are still in private hands. Some organisations also issued certificates to individual soldiers or next of kin to confirm the inclusion in the list. Some towns even issued commemorative medals for all who served.

GENERAL BIBLIOGRAPHY
BOOKS USEFUL IN FINDING RECORDS

(1) *Record Office Report 1982,* by John Rayment and Bill Taylor, FFHS.
(2) *Britain's Regimental Museums,* by Roy Batten, 199 Chiswick Village, London W4 3DG.
(3) *A Guide to Military Museums,* by Terence Wise, Athena Books, Doncaster, 1982.
(4) *British Archives and Sources for History of the World War,* by H. Hall, Oxford University Press, 1925. Reference Room Shelf, PRO, Kew. This contains an appendix listing the results of a survey on CROs in 1922. The original report is also in the PRO (reference unknown).
(5) *The Two World Wars: A Guide to Manuscript Collections in the UK,* by S.L. Mayer and W.J. Koenig, Bowker, 1976. A survey of CRO and other repositories in 1975. Reference Room Shelf, PRO, Kew, Book 25, Press 13.
(6) *A Bibliographic Guide to the Two World Wars,* by Gwyn M. Bayliss, Bowker, 1977. An annotated survey of English Language Reference Materials.
(7) *A Subject Bibliography of the First World War,* by A.G.S. Enser, Andre Deutsch. Lists books by subject, town name, Battle, unit and type of unit. Use with care; some entries have been found which do not appear to match the subject heading.
(8) *Bibliography of Regimental Histories of the British Army* by A.S. White. Covers all periods before and after 1914–18. Does not include memoirs and similar books. There are few Rolls of Honour.
(9) *British Military Museums and Events in the Silver Jubilee Year,* English Tourist Board, 1977.
(10) *British Union Catalogue of Periodicals,* by James D. Stewart and others, Butterworth Scientific Publications, 1956, available from most large reference libraries. A guide to the whereabouts of Regimental Magazines and Journals. Look first under Great Britain — Army — Corps — Regiment. This will refer you to the actual title of the journal. Also gives repositories which hold a complete set of each periodical.
(11) *British (Museum) Library Printed Book Catalogue,* published at intervals. Each of the many supplements has to be checked. WWI appears as 'European War'. The date of publication of a book does not determine the edition of the catalogue in which it appears. It depends on when a copy reached the Library.
(12) *A Guide to the Sources of British Military History,* edited by Robin Higham, Routledge and Kegan Paul.
(13) *Official Histories: Essays and Bibliographies from around the World,* edited by Robin Higham, Kansas State University Library, Manhattan, Kansas, 1970.

(14) *The Location of British Army Records 1914–18,* by Norman Holding, FFHS, 3rd edn., 1991.

(15) *Lineage Book of the British Land Forces 1660–1978,* Vols. 1 and 2, by J.B.M. Frederick, Microform Academic Publisher.

General Histories

For a more complete list, see *WWI Army Ancestry* by Norman Holding, FFHS, 3rd edn., 1997.

The British Army: A Concise History, by J. Haswell, Thomas and Hudson, 1975.

History of the First World War, by B.G. Liddell Hart, Pan Books, 1972.

Military Operations: France and Belgium, Vols. 1–14, by Brigadier-General Sir James E. Edmonds, part of the 'Official History' series).

Researching British Airmen of the Great War, by Andrew Whitmarsh, in *The Western Front Association Bulletin,* June 1998. A list of sources giving names of airmen, including Royal Flying Corps, Royal Naval Air Service and the RAF.

USEFUL RECORDS
IN THE PUBLIC RECORD OFFICE

Those containing names of men or women shown * (PRO Kew)

*	Medical Records	MH106/1 et seq.
	War Establishments	WO24/900 et seq.
	Army Council Instructions	WO293/1 et seq.
	Draft of Official Histories	CAB44; CAB45
	Embarkation Dates	WO162/7; WO33/763; WO25/3535 et seq.
	* Women Motor Drivers	WO162/62
	Monthly Returns	WO73/97–111
	Allocation Tables	WO95/5494
	ASC History	W161/12–13; W161/30; WO95/5466
	War Diaries	WO95/1 et seq.
	Orders of Battle	WO95/5467–70
	Orders of Battle, Russia	WO33/911
	Orders of Battle, Home Division	WO33/795
	War Maps	WO153/...
	Weekly Returns UK	WO114/25–56
	UK Units 1914 TF	WOl58/927–932
*	Part Nominal Roll QMAAC	WO162/16
	List of ACIs Re Volunteer Training Corps (extracts from WO293/...)	WO161/ 109
	Army Pay Corps Precedent Book (lists small training schools)	WO113/6
*	Army Discharge Papers 1900–13	WO97/5139
*	Royal Ordnance Corps Orders some lists of men	WO111/13
	Lists of units in named battles	WO161/103
	War Office papers – approx 20,000 files on every aspect of Army organisation. Very few names	WO32/...
	Lists of Nurses Arriving in France	WO95/3982
	War Diary of Deputy Director of Medical Services (DDMS) of Line of Communications	
	Recruiting Details (numbers not names)	WO162/6

	List of R.E. and R.A. Units with formation details	WO162/5 and 6
*	Naval men in the Armoured Car Convoy in Russia	ADM116/1717
	Lists of Ships (Troop or otherwise) entering Le Havre	WO95/4035
	War Diaries of 63rd Naval Div.	ADM137/3063–3088
	Army Orders	WO123/...
*	Medal Rolls	WO329/...
*	Conscientious Objectors (Middlesex only)	MH47/136–141
	Service Records of Soldiers WO363/...; WO364/...	

ABBREVIATIONS

ADS	Advanced Dressing Station; a first aid post
APS	Army Postal Service
ASC	Army Service Corps; Royal Army Service Corps in 1919
AVS	Army Veterinary Service
BEF	British Expeditionary Force. The term used to describe the British Army in France
Bibl. ref.	Bibliographical reference
BL	British Library, London
CCS	Casualty Clearing Station; an 800-bed tented hospital run by a Royal Army Medical Corps unit
CO	Commanding Officer
CRO	County Record Office
DDMS	Deputy Director of Medical Services
Div.	Division; a unit of approximately 18,000 men
Divnl.	Divisional; attached to or concerned with a Division
FA	Field Ambulance; an RAMC unit, not a vehicle
FHS	Family History Society
GHQ	General Headquarters; used for both the location and organisation
HQ	Headquarters
HMSO	Her Majesty's Stationery Office (Government Bookshops).
IC	as in 'Officer IC'. The Officer in Command of the unit
IWM	Imperial War Museum, London
L of C	Lines of Communication
MAC	Motor Ambulance Convoy; an RAMC unit
MGC	Machine Gun Corps
NAM	National Army Museum
NCO	Non-Commissioned Officer, i.e. Sergeant or Corporal
PRO	Public Record Office; all records referred to are at Kew
RA	Royal Artillery (known colloquially as The Gunners)
RAMC	Royal Army Medical Corps
RE	Royal Engineers (known colloqwally as The Sappers)
RN	Royal Navy
RAOC	Royal Army Ordnance Corps
TF, TA	Territorial Force, Territonal Army
WWI, WWII	World War I, World War II